Promotion and Marketing for Shopping Centers

A Basic Approach

S. Albert Wenner

International Council of Shopping Centers

ISBN: 0-913598-13-5
Library of Congress Catalog Card Number: 79-92291

Printed in the United States of America

ABOUT THE AUTHOR

S. Albert Wenner's wide and varied experience in the retail arena uniquely qualifies him as the author of a book on shopping center marketing and promotion. His insights stem from responsibilities as a store manager, district supervisor, fashion merchandiser, and sales promotion executive for Lerner Shops, the national fashion chain.

Mr. Wenner founded the sales promotion department for Lerner Shops almost 25 years ago and, as vice president for promotion, he was responsible for company participation in innumerable promotional programs of shopping centers where Lerner Shops were tenants.

He pioneered many of the techniques and events used by marketing directors today. Mr. Wenner is a frequent lecturer and panelist at industry meetings and conferences. He has also served from the beginning as a judge of ICSC's Maxi Awards, and in fact coined the name for this industrywide effort to evaluate and recognize significant shopping center promotion and marketing programs.

Mr. Wenner retired from Lerner Shops at the end of 1978. He is active as an instructor at the Fashion Institute of Technology, a retail consultant for both shopping centers and retail establishments, and is a frequent speaker at shopping center merchants association meetings.

CONTENTS

FOREWORD

Shopping centers have changed the course of retailing during the last quarter century in many ways. They brought retailers to the suburbs, they arranged for them to operate in an entirely new type of physical and selling environment, and helped them to become more profitable than they had ever been.

The most important thing about a shopping center is its stores. The proper mixture and balance of retailers properly presented attracts customers to the center as a whole. To let customers know what they can find in a center so that they will want to come to it to buy is the responsibility and objective of the sales promotion/marketing director.

No aspect of shopping centers has undergone such dramatic changes in the last few years as the art and science of sales promotion and marketing. Today's marketing director employs increasingly sophisticated and professional skills to help increase center sales. Many of the techniques and most of the tools developed over the years are set forth for the first time in this excellent handbook.

Shopping center sales promotion as a profession originated with the earliest centers after World War II, but it gained stability, identity and general acceptance with the inception of ICSC's Accredited Shopping Center Promotion Director (ASPD) program in 1971. Under this program, marketing leaders began to codify and define standards for the industry to apply and to measure professional performance.

S. Albert Wenner, the author of this book, is one of the pioneers in shopping center marketing. He approaches the field, not from the developer's bullpen but from the retailer's dugout. He hits a long and hard ball and has a champion lifetime record.

He has had more than 40 years of experience in retailing, the last 24 as advertising and promotion director of Lerner Shops. His vast knowledge and expertise come from personal involvement in merchant association and store promotion activities in more than 400 shopping centers.

As he says in his introduction, the essence of shopping center marketing is constant change. New theories and techniques are being developed and old ones adjusted to new conditions. In this manual Mr. Wenner sets forth the basic principles of organization, budgeting, advertising, publicity, promotion, special and merchandising events, media selection, research, and customer and community relations, all designed to increase center sales. He also introduces many of the new techniques now being tested within the industry from which will surely come new advances and achievements in an exciting, ever-changing, always challenging profession.

Albert Sussman

Executive Vice President
International Council of Shopping Centers

April 1980

INTRODUCTION

BASIC PRINCIPLES FOR SHOPPING CENTER MARKETING

The successful marketing of a shopping center is a complex task that must follow a careful plan. Reduced to its simplest common denominator, the goal of the plan is to produce profit for the center's tenants and owner. And profit, for a retail entity like a shopping center, comes from the sale of merchandise.

All of the elements of the plan must be thought out well in advance. They should represent a coordinated effort among all of the center's merchants, and be directed specifically at the customers in the center's trade area. A good plan goes beyond advertising, sales promotion and presenting a series of special events. It avoids "backing into" a program using a trial and error approach. Instead, it is a deliberate series of actions taken to bring a center to its potential volume and beyond.

The concept of positioning is at the foundation of a successful marketing plan. Positioning means more than creating a favorable image of a center in its customers' minds, although this is a key ingredient. The marketing/promotion director must carefully analyze the center's strengths and weaknesses (including in the assessment such factors as location, tenant mix, architecture, and ease of accessibility) and devote the same care to determining competitors' strengths and weaknesses. To be successful, the marketing program must capitalize on the center's strengths and the competitors' weaknesses.

In addition to determining the position a center should take in its market (a conclusion based on research of the trade area; see Chapter 2), the marketing/promotion director must always keep in mind certain basic principles that will ensure that the program is well-funded, cohesive, and includes the participation of the majority of tenants.

There are dangers inherent in putting forth a series of principles for a project as entrepreneurial and as reflective of individual circumstances as a modern shopping center. Each project must stand on its own, and the degree to which each point in the plan is accepted must depend entirely on individual circumstances. Therefore, the principles set forth below should be regarded as basic guidelines and not irrevocable dictums. Nonetheless, the unity and sense of purpose they foster can produce meaningful results—in sales and profits—for virtually all shopping centers.

While the nine principles are written from the standpoint of the new center, they are applicable, with relatively minor adjustments, to the older center undergoing expansion, modernization and enclosure. The latter is an area in which major attention is now being paid, and the marketing/promotion director of an older project is well-advised to capitalize upon the opportunity to improve the center's role in its marketplace.

The semantic and scheduling differences aside between a "Grand Opening" and a "Grand

Reopening," the challenges and opportunities to be gained from researching, planning, shaping, and implementing a center's marketing plan remain the same, and the guidelines below transcend all other differences.

Principle 1. All new shopping centers must, no less than six months before opening, institute a continuing, aggressive publicity program. The promotion/marketing director or an agency skilled in shopping center promotion and publicity must be available to plan and execute this important preopening phase. The same planning and care should also go into a preopening plan for a renovation or expansion.

Principle 2. All shopping centers must have an operating merchants association, or a steering committee of merchants if structured as a promotion fund, at least three months prior to the opening, but preferably six months to a year in advance. Membership or contributions to the fund should be mandated by lease, and participation by all tenants is essential if they are to derive the maximum benefit from marketing activities. Although the promotional fund does away with a formalized association and bylaws and may not exhibit the same problems that arise when dealing with a merchants association, for the purposes of this principle the merchants association and the promotional funds are interchangeable.

Principle 3. All shopping center promotional activity must be developed and implemented by the center's marketing director or agency. However, it is subject, in principle, to the approval of the merchants association membership, the board of directors, and/or the promotion committee, as specified in the bylaws if the center is operating with a merchants association. (If the promotion fund concept is in effect, the marketing director approves on behalf of the developer.)

Principle 4. All stores in the shopping center must be promoted as a single cohesive unit, not as individual components within one area. In short, the image of a shopping center as a horizontal department store must be established and maintained.

Principle 5. All shopping center print advertising for specific promotions must appear as a unit, fronted by a center-sponsored page that uses a cohesive theme. Advertising by individual merchants then follows, with all ads stressing the same theme.

Principle 6. Events presented on radio or television should follow the same guidelines—they should promote all stores as a unit and use an identical theme. All merchant-purchased spots should have the shopping center theme as a lead-in unit or tag line, with the individual store message using the remaining time.

Principle 7. Most merchandising events must be bolstered by a promotional "device" designed to further attract the public. Conversely, all major promotional devices should be coordinated with some type of merchandise promotion.

Principle 8. Every shopping center should be involved in community affairs through its financial support of major community endeavors, by sharing the use of shopping center facilities, by planning and participating in civic events, and so on. These activities build good will that translates into increased traffic to the center.

Principle 9. Strong lines of communication must be established and maintained between the center's promotional unit and the merchants.

All principles of the basic plan stress the importance of unanimity of action: promotion and marketing of a shopping center as a unit—a unit that will appeal to a specific trade area. Centers that adhere to this most basic tenet, that also have timely, aggressive promotions, and that are a part of the community will have the best opportunity to reach and maintain their volume potential.

MARKETING A SMALL CENTER WITH A SMALL BUDGET

The small shopping center, in numbers at least, is the foundation of the shopping center industry. Upwards of 75 percent of the centers in the United States are below 200,000 square feet in size. Even assuming such centers have an organized merchants association, probably scant attention is paid to anything more than a few tabloids issued in the course of the year and some decorations and a larger section issued in advance of the Christmas buying period. Store advertising may be sporadic.

Historically, even these relatively minor efforts require a coordinator. If the center has a property manager, he may double in spades on such activities. The developer may turn the organizing and coordination of efforts over to a small advertising/promotion agency in the area. The media, themselves, may have space or time salespeople available. Part-time promotional assistance can be employed. Lastly, if the developer/owner—or his managing agents—has several small centers in the same or nearby areas, he may assign a full-time person on staff to coordinate a multiple-center effort.

Whatever the solution, the obvious preexisting condition must be that the developer and the merchants recognize that there is a need for a promotional effort of some sort. A truism in the shopping center industry is that each center has a market and a cadre of customers (if it did not, there would be no tenants in the center and/or it would not have been built in the first place).

Even in small shopping centers, few developers and equally few retailers are willing to operate in a vacuum as it relates to promotion, marketing, and advertising. Assuming there is a commitment to promote, and the wherewithal to undertake an effort, the individual charged with the responsibility for that activity—however minimal—is not without resources.

Almost everything presented in these pages can be scaled down to smaller efforts, assuming of course that they fit in with the overall concept of the center. Participatory advertising—in which the merchants share a full page—can be employed to reduce costs for all. Weekly "shoppers" frequently sell small display space at low cost.

Local clubs and civic organizations are good sources of free promotional activity. Art shows, flower shows, and hobby and craft shows sponsored in conjunction with these groups are typical of many low-cost, no-cost events that can be arranged. When coordi-nated with merchandise offerings and advertising, these events can draw customers to a center. They are inexpensive because the clubs supply displays and center management need only supply that dash of imagination that will make the event a crowdpleaser. (Chapter 7 offers additional ideas for low-budget events.)

If the center's trade area is small, direct mail may be an effective way to reach customers. Flyers that announce coming events, reminders of merchandise specials, or even greeting cards can be sent to customers. For a small donation, members of Scout troops or high school clubs may be willing to help address envelopes.

Christmas—that all-important selling season—is a good time to spur merchants into cooperative efforts. The merchants can supply some of the decorations, and they may enjoy getting together to put them up. A coordinated theme for window decor at this time can give the center a unified look that will please customers. Finally, almost every merchant will be interested in advertising, so it would be possible to put together an attractive tabloid or cooperative ad.

These are just a few examples of what can be done on a limited budget. There are endless possibilities. The center manager or promotion/marketing director need not surrender because the promotion budget is small; instead, he or she can meet the challenge with persistence and originality.

To best portray our basic principles, we use Bel Air Shopping City, a hypothetical shopping center. Throughout the book, and most particularly in the appendix material, Bel Air is presented as the typical shopping center—one of the more than 19,000 throughout the United States and Canada that have become part of the most striking retail phenomenon of this century. These modern, attractive, convenient retail complexes constantly and aggressively reinforce their physical attributes through sound marketing and promotion.

To spur further thought about the concepts presented in the text, discussion questions are included at the end of each chapter. These questions encourage readers to expand upon the material in the chapter.

S. Albert Wenner

ACKNOWLEDGMENTS

This book is dedicated to my wife Joyce, whose enthusiastic support, continued encouragement, and wise counsel during the time needed to complete the book, made the difficult project much easier.

Thanks must also go to my children, Jamie and Scott, for their understanding when weekends and vacations that would normally have been spent with them were devoted instead to research and writing. Because of Joyce, Jamie, and Scott, this is a finished book, not just an idea for one.

Special thanks to my good friends Spencer and Jack for their ongoing belief that it would be done, when it appeared that it could not, and to countless others who discussed the problems and suggested solutions, unselfishly shared their knowledge, and answered questions with the gift of their experience.

Finally, mention must be made of the contributions to this book by Larry Goodman, vice president, retail, Hank Simons, vice president, creative director, and Tom Clemente, art director, of the Newspaper Advertising Bureau, the association of the newspaper advertising industry. Mr. Goodman thoughtfully reviewed the chapter on advertising, and his comments were most helpful. The NAB team also developed a graphic approach for our hypothetical shopping center that combines the best elements of merchandising art and advertising. These roughs represent the kind of graphics that all centers, new and old, can well emulate and adapt, in concept and approach.

S. A. W.

1

THE MERCHANTS ASSOCIATION OR PROMOTION FUND: WHERE IT ALL BEGINS

From the first time a group of retail merchants shared a common location or facility, discussion ensued on how to put their collective best feet forward to maximize their sales potential. Their rationale for joint action was simple—how else could individually owned and operated stores, each with its own merchandising approaches, attempt to coexist side-by-side and hope to prosper? The early response of urban merchants was to form chambers of commerce, primarily voluntary, since there was no common landlord to organize or to mandate membership. The same rationale lay behind shopping center merchants' efforts to organize, and since the early 1950s virtually every shopping center of size and substance has had some form of organization of its merchants.

The merchants association was never intended to replace the individual promotional capabilities of merchants, and, spirited as they are, merchants did not immediately embrace the developer's concept of an association and then eschew individual promotion and advertising solely in favor of cooperative ventures.

In fact, there were, and still are, some merchants who oppose joining an association. For the most part, the nonjoiners represent the two extremes of retailers—the very large, who have no need to depend on promotion efforts other than their own, and the very small, whose budgets and operations probably preclude meaningful participation in joint efforts.

Virtually all shopping centers being developed today, and a majority of those that have opened within the last 30 years and that are large enough to sustain regular promotional activity (even as minimal as Christmas decorations) have a form of mandatory merchants association. Promotion funds, a more recent development, are assuming a steadily increasing role and are, in fact, replacing merchant associations in many new centers.

Dues in a merchants association or promotion fund vary widely, as does the manner of collection. Equally variable is the degree to which the owner-developer contributes to the activities.

Granting these variables, a basic assumption is made in this book—that the developer of the center and the merchants who will be in this shopping center recognize that an aggressive, enthusiastic marketing program is the single most important element of shopping center promotion. This program may rest in the hands of a professional marketing director or, as is often the case, it may be developed through the efforts of a marketing/promotion director working in conjunction with the merchants association or steering committee.

After years of trial and error, an almost standard format for organizing a merchants association has emerged. Promotion funds, while of more recent vintage, are nearly uniform in structure as well, having benefited from the merchants association experience that evolved over the years. While there are variations in different locales, the plan detailed below can outline the formation of a strong, imaginative association that will function intelligently and effectively.

WHEN TO ORGANIZE A MERCHANTS ASSOCIATION

Obviously, the first step in the formation of an association is the developer's recognition that there is a need for one, coupled with a provision in the leases or reciprocal operating agreements that all merchants will join. Most lease agreements specify that an association will be formed, that the merchants agree to join and pay a pro-rata share of the expenses of the association, that the developer will provide a specified percentage of the annual costs, that the developer and tenants also will pay a specified amount of the preopening and opening costs, and that bylaws, personnel, detailed programs, and budgets will be developed at later dates and in time for the first organizational meeting of the association.

From the developer's point of view, this agreement constitutes assurance that there will be a merchants association and provides ample time to fully plan how the center will be promoted. Retailers, as well, have key assurances—that all merchants will be tied together in a common merchandising and promotion effort, that the developer will pay a fair share, that both the developer and tenants will have a say in how the association is structured and will function, and, lastly, that the views of the participants will be heard as they relate to personnel, types of promotions, budgets, and schedules.

With such lease assurances, and with construction under way, the developer can begin preopening promotion. At this early stage, it is usually the development firm that takes the initiative in organizing and planning. No later than three months before opening, and preferably six months or longer in advance of opening, the merchants association should begin to be a functioning entity. A marketing director or agency appointed by the developer should be formulating basic plans and approaches—copylines, graphics, schedules, and programs—for the opening and immediate postopening period. Such plans are usually put forth at the first organizational meeting, when official bylaws are formally adopted. It is at this stage that the association truly begins to take shape, to formulate policy, to approve opening plans and budgets, and to voice its opinions on the myriad details that go into creating a successful opening.

Appendix A contains basic announcement forms, response cards, sample language, and a typical agenda for the first organizational meeting of the association.

As stated earlier, most leases now mandate the membership of stores in a merchants association. *Active members* are those with businesses, service organizations, or professional offices located in the center who will benefit from the efforts of the association. A second form of membership—*associate*—often is extended to corporations, partnerships, or individuals who, in the opinion of the majority of the board, have interests and goals in common with active members. Associate members might include companies handling the center's maintenance, security, and landscaping, or occupants of office space within the center who do not benefit directly from promotional efforts and the like. Entitled to attend membership meetings, they usually do not have the right to vote on association matters, although their views are often valuable for the entire center.

At the first organizational meeting, it is important to inaugurate and sustain a common effort for the common objective—namely, the promotion of the shopping center as an entity. To conceive a course by which this goal is to be reached is the province of the marketing director; it is the association's board of directors who espouse or alter this course; and eventually the entire association will endorse it. At this point, the concept of a shopping center as a horizontal department store is most evident. In a vertical department store an advertising or special events director will conceive an idea, it will be presented to and "bought" by store management, and then left to individual departments and their personnel to implement in terms of merchandise, displays, and the like. With this analogy in mind, let's proceed to the basics of organizing an association.

BYLAWS

The lease document gives birth to the merchants association, but the bylaws give it shape, form, purpose, and meaning. Prepared well in advance of the merchants association formation meeting, the bylaws are the constitution by which shopping centers operate. Although specific provisions within the bylaws differ from center to center, their purpose is always identical—unanimity of action for promoting the center. Bylaws are best developed and written by an individual or an agency with experience in center operations and promotion. They should define every item necessary for the guidance of the governing body and for the implementation of promotional programs. The developer and the agency or individual developing the bylaws must meet before the bylaws are prepared to discuss the inclusion of specific items and conditions. A draft of the bylaws should be available well in advance of their publication, and they must be approved by lawyers before they are printed.

Appendix B presents three samples of bylaws. Although language and, in some instances, procedures vary, their intent is to provide a vehicle for planning, developing, and executing promotions, publicity, involvement in community affairs, and all other projects that will increase customer traffic to the shopping center, which will, in turn, ensure benefits for all tenants.

However, there are some areas of potential conflict that must be eliminated. The first step is to be certain that terms used throughout the bylaws are defined and clarified at the first organizational meeting, or soon thereafter. The following points are particularly important.

There should be a clear distinction between the *opening period* and the subsequent *fiscal year*. Because separate assessments are usually paid for each of the two periods, the starting and cut-off dates must be stated so there

will be no possibility of misunderstanding. Usually the opening period starts with the preopening publicity and continues for 30 days after the Grand Opening. The Grand Opening assessment is usually the equivalent of six months' to one year's merchants association dues. The details of the length of the Grand Opening period, the date at which the assessment is due, and the specific amount due are spelled out in each merchant's lease, and may vary from developer to developer.

The fiscal year starts immediately after the opening period has ended. Tenants whose stores are still not ready to open start to pay dues when they open for business. Although dues are prorated in most instances, late-opening tenants often are obligated to pay for the entire quarter during which they opened. Because they benefited from the preopening and Grand Opening promotions for which they pay no dues, a charge for the entire quarter can be justified.

What follows are explanations of specific sections of the bylaws coupled with a discussion of the rationale behind them and the techniques utilized to help establish a well-coordinated, efficient organization.

Assessments

Payment formulas for all tenants are spelled out in the lease. The generally accepted formula for assessment uses a computation of gross area occupied by categories of tenants. Thus, department stores usually pay less per square foot than supermarkets or junior department stores with substantially less space, and the latter will, in turn, have smaller per-square-foot assessments than other tenants that occupy still smaller areas. Specific square foot assessments can vary widely based on the area and the cost of advertising and promotion. New leases have a dues structure that ranges from 35 to more than 50 cents per square foot; and depending on the locale, the rate of inflation, and media costs, even higher dues can be expected in the immediate future. In addition, many leases link subsequent increases in association or promotion fund dues to changes in the Consumer Price Index.

The owner-developer also is obligated by terms of the lease to make a contribution that is based on the aggregate amount paid by all merchants. The developer's assessment also varies, but it is usually one-quarter to one-third of the total. Thus, if the dues paid by all tenants is $120,000, the developer would add $30,000 or $40,000 to this sum, increasing the available merchants association funds to $150,000 or $160,000.

Another formula in use bases the dues structure on the various levels occupied by tenants; the street-floor assessment thus has the highest base per square foot, with other floors having proportionately lower rates. Still another method of computing dues uses front footage together with the gross area occupied.

Finally, there is also a graduated dues structure based on the gross area occupied. The following dues schedule is an example, although this practice is followed only in a limited number of shopping centers:

First 1,000 square feet of gross area leased–$.40 per square foot
Next 1,500 square feet of gross area leased–$.35 per square foot
Next 2,500 square feet of gross area leased–$.30 per square foot
Next 2,500 square feet of gross area leased–$.22 per square foot
Next 5,000 square feet of gross area leased–$.18 per square foot
Next 5,000 square feet of gross area leased–$.14 per square foot
Next 10,000 square feet of gross area leased–$.12 per square foot
Next 22,500 square feet of gross area leased–$.08 per square foot
Over 50,000 square feet of gross area leased–$.04 per square foot

The gross-area method of assessment by categories is used by the majority of centers. It is an equitable and easily understood formula, and is usually acceptable to large and small tenants alike.

Grand Opening assessments are always in addition to dues paid for the first fiscal year, which begins immediately after the designated opening period. The structure for dues is usually the same for both cycles, and the square foot amounts for the Grand Opening are generally similar to those paid for the fis-

cal year, although this varies and could be anywhere from one-half to an equivalent sum. Local circumstances, such as a strongly competitive nearby center, temporary delays in fully completing access roads to the center, or the failure of an anchor and other stores to open, usually dictate adjustments in opening period expenditures.

In unusual circumstances, the budget and assessments must necessarily be increased to meet additional expenditures. If the dues structure written into the leases does not provide sufficient funds, the bylaws usually permit a special assessment. On occasion, however, the owner-developer and the major stores will make the extra contributions necessary to bridge the deficit.

METHODS OF PAYMENT AND BUDGET PLANNING

Dues for the fiscal year, which is effective 30 days after the opening period ends, are payable in advance upon presentation of an invoice. Tenants are billed differently by different centers, based on accounting systems and needs. In addition, requests for payment in advance on an annual, semiannual, quarterly, or even a monthly basis are often made. From a retailer's point of view, quarterly contributions are usually the most acceptable. Quarterly payment makes funds available to meet current planned budget expenditures and emergency situations, and also permits better supervision and control of the budget than would be possible if dues were paid semiannually or annually.

To expedite payment and to avoid a loss of time, a detailed budget covering the period for which the dues are requested should be made available to all tenants in advance of the billing. The expenditure of merchants association funds is usually planned for the entire fiscal year, allocated on a monthly basis, and reported to tenants annually, semiannually, or quarterly. The published budget informs the general membership about the use of their dues, while substantiating planned expenditures.

ASSOCIATION MEETINGS

Periodic meetings of the entire membership are always stipulated in the bylaws and are most necessary. It is at these meetings that directors and officers are elected, the budget is approved or amended, and all other business requiring a vote of the general membership is handled. The dates and site of the general membership meetings are stated in the bylaws, with provisions for postponement if necessary.

The date of the meeting at which directors and officers are elected and the annual budget is approved is usually designated in the bylaws. Many merchants associations use the occasion for a yearly dinner or cocktail party, and the expenses are paid from merchants associations monies or by the owner-developer. However, usually only two or three key people from each organization are invited and attend. Appendix C displays a sample invitation. Invitations should reach guests at least four to five weeks before the meeting.

The number of general membership meetings varies by center. Some centers schedule only annual meetings for elections and budget approval. In these instances, emergency meetings can be held as required. Other centers have semiannual or quarterly meetings, as specified in the bylaws. The preferred schedule in most centers is twice annually. This permits a review of the budget for the coming six months, a vote on matters requiring general membership approval, and discussion of unresolved problems. Most important, the meetings provide an opportunity to enhance communications among tenants as well as between owner and tenants. This is a key factor in contributing to the effective implementation of the promotional program and to the judicious use of merchants associations funds.

COMMITTEES

Forming committees for the administration of the merchants association is one way to delegate responsibility and to oversee the day-to-day operations of this important organization. Committee members are usually appointed by the association president, with the concurrence of the board of directors. They may serve for a one-year term or for as long as the board decides. Committees or committee members cannot allocate merchants association funds to any project without the written approval of the board of directors. The efforts of these committees are usually coordinated by the marketing director.

An alternative to the committee system is to give the marketing director, with the approval of the board of directors, the authority to act independently in the name of the merchants association. Because the purpose of the merchants association is to present the shopping center as a single merchandising entity, for the benefit of all, many centers have found that a strong, capable, professional marketing director can better perform all of the functions described below for the committees. If this alternative is chosen, the only committees needed are the nominating committee to elect officers, and the executive committee which sets policy.

Executive Committee

This committee consists of the president, vice-president, secretary, and treasurer. Between meetings it is the voice of the association.

Promotion Committee

The promotion committee does not develop the promotional programs, but it is available to the marketing director for advice and consultation during the development stage. It is usually comprised of a small group of merchants representing a cross section of the tenants. The advice of this group can be particularly helpful when scheduling events.

Nominating Committee

Five members of the merchants association appointed by the president usually serve as the nominating committee. This committee handles all details of the nominations to the association's board of directors. The bylaws state the specific procedures for nominations, and the committee is responsible for seeing that these procedures are followed when nominations are made.

Community Relations Committee

This committee usually consists of three to five association members, frequently with local tenants rather than department-store or chain-store representatives in the majority. Such a balance can provide the opportunity for greater community involvement, more knowledgeable direction, and easier rapport with community leaders. This committee is concerned with charitable contributions, use of the community room, if there is one, involvement in specific local affairs, and any other matters that relate to and contribute to community good will. The community relations program that evolves is implemented by the marketing director or agency, after presentation and approval by the board of the general membership, as specified in the bylaws.

Other committees may be appointed by the president, with the approval of the board of directors, to handle special situations as the need arises.

BOARD OF DIRECTORS

Directors are elected at the annual general membership meeting as stipulated in the bylaws. The board usually includes a representative of the owner-developer as well as seats for all anchor stores. This allocation of membership, particularly to the department stores, is judicious because it assures their interest and influence in the affairs of the merchants association. The balance of board membership is made up of chain stores and local merchants.

The total number of board members determines the numerical majority, and the owner-developer and department stores usually vote as a bloc. They are often joined by one or more chain or local stores, which invariably assures their having an active role in promotion activities. Many centers actually write their bylaws to provide for a majority of directors to be from among chain and local stores, thus avoiding accusations that the merchants association is controlled by the owner-developer and the anchor stores.

Merchants associations frequently split into large-store and small-store blocs. The large stores often want to dominate the coordination and timing of merchandise promotions, special events, media selection, and expenditure of the budget. The chains and smaller local stores may have opposing points of view, and an impasse results. Either group may then refuse to participate in center-sponsored activities that are being financed from merchants association funds to which they contributed.

Because the anchor stores normally draw most of the traffic and spend substantial amounts on consistent newspaper, radio, and television advertising, they expect other merchants to follow their promotion lead. Quite obviously, every center-sponsored event will be stronger with the participation of all merchants, large and small alike. It is to help gain this unanimity that the bylaws frequently specify that representatives from chain and small stores make up a numerical majority on the board of directors, with the balance of the seats held by the department stores and the owner-developer, as discussed above. Constitutionally, the small stores have control over the board of directors, but realistically a swing of one or two votes, which are usually readily available, gives anchor stores the practical majority in certain circumstances.

It is unrealistic to expect that all merchants associations function smoothly at all times. Political in-fighting, personal egos, store policies, the ability and personality of the marketing director, and the developer's own view all have a direct bearing on how the association functions. These are among the reasons why there has been a drift away from formal associations and toward promotion funds. The trend toward promotion funds is gaining considerable impetus, and has been adopted by several large developers.

OFFICERS

Officers always include a president, vice-president, secretary, and treasurer. In some instances an assistant secretary and assistant treasurer are part of the group. The principal officers are directors of the merchants association and are elected to their posts by the board. The assistant secretary and/or treasurer are not directors and are usually appointed by the president after his or her election.

As in any corporation, the officers make decisions and conduct the day-to-day business of the merchants association. Their operations must, of course, be in accordance with the bylaws of the corporation, and many decisions are subject to approval by the general membership.

There are no firm, inflexible rules or standards that apply to tenant representation among the officers. Ideally, they should have knowledge of the area, of the idiosyncrasies of the market, of the correct timing of events, and of the shopping habits of potential center visitors. In any circumstances, among the officers there should be included one or two anchor stores, national chain stores, and local merchants.

However the details of the establishment of the merchants association are worked out, the association should always work to promote cooperation among landlord and tenants. The overriding goal of the association is the creation and maintenance of a cohesive, coordinated promotion/marketing program that enhances the horizontal department store image of the center.

THE FIRST MEETING

The formation meeting of the association serves a utilitarian purpose—namely, to get the organization under way. Almost as important, however, are the impressions that the first meeting creates in terms of the overall plans for the center's merchandising and promotion push, the evaluation of the marketing director's creativity and skill, and the degree to which the merchants will work together for their individual and collective good. The person organizing that first meeting must always bear in mind that for most of the merchants this will be the first time they have met as a group.

It is for this reason that most development companies attempt to make this meeting a combined business and social function. Frequently wives are invited and, more often than not for regional shopping centers, the event is built around a cocktail hour and sit-down dinner.

Special care should be taken to make it a gracious event, free from rancor and dissent. The promotion/marketing director will be well advised to communicate in advance with selected merchants, particularly anchor stores, to bounce off ideas, get a "feel" of their views, and explain possibly controversial aspects of the organization, program, and budget.

It is a good idea to add a little showmanship to all merchants association meetings. If the merchants are bored with the presentation of the year's promotion plans, they are unlikely to support the program enthusiastically. A little showmanship can spark interest, and ensure support.

When to Schedule, Whom to Invite

Notices of the meeting should be sent out as far in advance as possible, and certainly no later than a month before the scheduled event. Invitations should go to the key person at the headquarters of the anchor stores and to the home offices of the chains as well as to the principals of local stores and service stores. The question of which individual to invite is best determined in consultation with the developer, the developer's leasing staff, or with the person who executed the lease for the tenant. Each store representative must, however, have the authority to vote on the proposals and approve the basic bylaw document.

The bylaws and any supporting data should be mailed, at least two weeks before the meeting, to all tenants who are attending with a request that they be reviewed and that any troublesome areas be discussed in advance of the meeting. This simple technique can serve to provide tenants with a sense of participation and can help assure speedier approval and a minimum of dissent.

Accompanying the bylaws should be an agenda for the meeting. Some marketing directors supply a copy of the preliminary preopening and Grand Opening budget and sufficient details to provide tenants with a glimpse of what is proposed. Frequently, this can work to the marketing director's disadvantage, because all merchants have ideas and all merchants lay claim to being experts in publicity and promotion. There is no rule for determining how much in-depth material should be provided in advance. To a large degree it is linked to timing of the meeting; the closer the meeting is held to the opening date, the more material must be provided.

The most successful preopening organizational meetings are carefully staged and meticulous in their organization and structure, providing basic documentation at times calculated to have maximum impact. This is not to say that the meeting must be engineered and "fixed," but rather that it must be far more than a casual necessity if it is to be effective.

Equal care should go into determining the site of the meeting. A hotel or restaurant near the new shopping center with the business portion of the meeting preceded by a cocktail hour and dinner has proven to be effective.

In summary, the important details that should be presented at this meeting include:

1. Preopening budget—promotion expense and planning four to six weeks prior to and extending 30 days beyond the Grand Opening.
2. Merchants association articles of incorporation.
3. Merchants association bylaws—a duplicate of those mailed previously.
4. Logo—in various sizes with instructions for its use.
5. Fact sheet—including the center's address, which shows identifying roads and highways, store hours, *employee* parking regulations, lighting requirements, trash removal, delivery hours, and maintenance plans. Also included should be all pertinent facts relating to the center: the owner-developer, architect, builder, center management and promotion staff, as well as all the details that will be informative and helpful to the tenants.
6. Tenant listing—including a floor plan identifying by matching number the locations of all the occupants.

The Grand Opening

A subject often discussed in depth at the first organizational meeting, but often decided upon at a later meeting, is the Grand Opening—specific plans as well as budget and funding.

As outlined earlier, usually there are two budgets for the new center: the fiscal year budget, which starts 30 days after the grand opening period and covers the full year, and the Grand Opening budget, to support the plans, giveaways, programs, and events that make up the preopening and Grand opening period and for the ensuing 30 days.

As a general rule of thumb, most Grand Opening budgets range from 50 to 100 percent of the annual assessment and budget. The latter figure is particularly true in the case of major centers entering into an area where retail competition already exists and the center

must make an immediate, hard-hitting impact on the buying public.

Also influencing this budget are factors such as media costs and effectiveness, date of the center opening, type of center, lease and association requirements, as well as the degree of developer and anchor store financial support.

Participation of all tenants in the Grand Opening promotion usually is mandatory. Tenant assessments and developer contributions follow the same formula outlined in the lease. This enables the marketing director to accurately project the amount of money that will be available, and gives him or her the financial assurance to develop a strong, effective opening plan. In some instances, developers have been known to go beyond their lease requirements and augment the promotional fund. Concomitantly, although most anchors recognize the importance of a grand opening and will contribute to it, not all anchor stores are required by their lease or operating agreement to contribute. This sometimes occurs where an anchor store has been operating on the site for some time prior to the official Grand Opening or in cases where a shopping center is built around an existing anchor store.

While establishment of this financial support is beyond the involvement of the marketing director (usually it is written in the original real estate deal), it is not beyond the director to at least encourage a recalcitrant anchor store to participate in the Grand Opening through in-kind contributions—advertising in a special section, adoption of the basic promotion theme, developing special merchandising events, and the like.

With the merchants association now a functioning entity (having been created at the organizational meeting), details of the Grand Opening are best left to the marketing director working with the association board of directors or promotion committee. As in all dealings with merchants, it is essential to develop a regular series of communications to keep them abreast of what is happening and what is expected of them. Some centers even hold a series of meetings to deal specifically with the Grand Opening as a way of assuring that each merchant is kept informed and is thereby able to put the best foot forward at this most important of all shopping center events.

In point of fact, the planning for the Grand Opening ideally should have begun the moment a marketing director or agency was assigned to the task of developing an overall promotion approach and to undertake the preopening publicity and events. Also, the Grand Opening should logically reflect all that has transpired beforehand and build on the plus factors that were discussed in the preopening stages—the community advantages, the depth of shopping, the free and easy accessiblity, the locale. The marketing experts will rely on the predevelopment consumer survey and market research results to find the new center's position.

Collecting funds for the Grand Opening promotion and activities also must start well in advance. If the organizational meeting of the association was held six months prior to opening, all tenants must be made aware of plans and be billed for their pro-rata shares of the opening costs three to four months in advance. If the organizational meeting was held only three months prior to opening, then at least two months lead time must be devoted to organizing and collecting funds for the opening. The promotion director who expects to start the collection of opening assessments in the 30 days prior to center's opening shows a lack of knowledge of the way most retail firms operate and ignores the fact that they are busy putting the final touches on their stores.

It should go without saying that for centers that have no lease requirements for funding the Grand Opening, six months before the opening is none too soon to begin contacting tenants and persuading them to support the event on a fixed assessment schedule, preferably at least 50 percent or more of the annual assessment. The gamut of ways to persuade tenants must be used in such instances— letters, telephone calls, personal visits, including to chain-store home offices if need be—to achieve the desired 100 percent participation.

Funds allocated and assessed for the Grand Opening are usually budgeted to cover preopening promotion expenses, and expenses incurred during the subsequent 30 days. This extended promotional period provides continuity, so that the momentum generated by the preopening and Grand Opening activities will be fed by ongoing publicity and promotion for an additional month.

Continued drum-beating during the immediate postopening period strongly influences the formulation of shopping habits that will continue for many years. The promotional program will have reached its absolute peak during the several days preceding and through the center's opening. At this point, after the Grand Opening period, while the pace of promotional activity will decrease, it remains constant through the 30-day period following the opening.

During the preopening period, much of the merchants association promotional funds will have been allocated for radio, television (as the budget permits), and institutional image-building newspaper advertising. Starting with the several days immediately preceding the Grand Opening, emphasis should be transferred from image-building to merchandising. Immediately after the opening, the necessity for ongoing publicity and promotion cannot be overstated. Continuing emphasis must be placed on the basics: location, identified by roads and highways that bound the center; opening and closing store hours; the availability of adequate free parking; the merchant mix; and so on. These facts should be emphasized again and again.

Having completed the preopening, Grand Opening, and postopening periods, the shopping center is now geared for normal, daily operations. The performance from this point on will be influenced by the impact made on the prime and secondary market areas during the opening promotion periods and, of course, the quality and strength of continuing promotional efforts.

PROMOTION FUNDS—THE ALTERNATIVE TO MERCHANTS ASSOCIATIONS

As noted in the preceding discussion, a dramatic change is occurring in the area of shopping center promotion and marketing as it relates to the functioning, control, and programming of promotional activities. The promotion fund arrangement is a relatively new technique that has been adopted by many major developers. It replaces the formal merchants association with a promotional unit appointed and controlled by the developer. A steering committee of merchants sometimes acts in an advisory capacity.

Although all of the results are not yet in, promotion funds now appear to be workable alternatives to merchants associations. Many of the characteristics of merchants associations also apply to promotion funds. Among these are the dues structure (grand opening and fiscal year) for tenants and developers, merchant meetings (including the first one for a discussion of grand opening plans), and committees.

The chief difference is that promotion funds are totally controlled and administered by the office of the developer, and the marketing director reports to and is answerable solely to the developer, rather than to an association of merchants. However, merchants continue to pay dues, as stipulated by leases, and the owner-developer contributes an amount usually equal to, or more than, the traditional 25 to 33-1/3 percent of the merchant total, and most operating costs remain pretty much the same.

The promotion fund is designed to enable the owner-developer greater flexibility in programming and implementing events as well as in effecting operating economies that make a greater portion of the promotion fund income available for promotional activities. Payment of promotional fees (i.e., dues) are mandated by lease, and fees are transmitted monthly to the owner-developer, along with common area and other charges, at the same time as rent. Because promotion fund amounts appear on a single invoice, the separate bookkeeping and billing functions necessary when a merchants association operates as an entity are eliminated. The newer, more efficient invoice system obviously reduces expenses.

Although the promotion fund is under the sole control of the owner-developer, a steering committee composed of merchant tenants is frequently appointed to provide advice and be available for consultation on matters relating to preparation of the budget, the timing of merchandise events and traffic-building devices, media selection, and so on. However, the steering committee operates in an advisory capacity only.

The fund is administered by the marketing director, appointed by the owner-developer, who also retains the authority over promotional personnel. This, in itself, has been cited by many professional marketing directors as a key advantage of promotional funds, since it frees the director from the myriad organizational details, interassociation politics, and rivalries, and permits greater concentration on marketing and promotion rather than on association details.

Leases with the promotion fund provision may contain a contingency clause that permits conversion into a conventional merchants association, to be invoked at the discretion of the owner-developer. When and if this were to occur, the promotion fund balance would be transferred to a newly organized merchants association, and that organization would simply assume the responsibility for all promotional activity in the center in accordance with bylaws promulgated prior to the changeover.

Many leases being executed today mandate a contribution to the promotion of the center but are open-ended in an organizational sense, giving the owner-developer the option to either organize a merchants association or develop a promotional fund. At the lease-signing stage, tenants are only obligated to financially participate in promotional activities.

Because merchant-tenants pay fees directly to the owner under the promotion fund concept and do not assume an active role in planning, the establishment and maintenance of clear lines of communication between owner-developer and tenant is imperative; without communication, tenant cooperation will fall by the wayside. This means discussion of the promotion program before it is made final; consultation on the timing of both merchandise events and traffic-building devices, as well as on the depth of expenditures for specific programs; and an opportunity to examine the budget before the fact. Often, this communication is made possible through the creation of a steering committee of merchants. At least one general meeting of tenants should be held each year, or semiannually, as a means to maintain contact with the entire merchant group, keep them informed, get their ideas, and review results.

In this way, center management would be making a goodwill gesture, but equally important, it would permit making use of available merchant guidance and input. As every developer and tenant knows, the name of the shopping center game is sales, which can be influenced upward or downward by the proper or improper timing of events and the degree of merchant cooperation.

Without prejudging the promotional fund's effectiveness, the delicate balance between promotion and merchandising calls for a blend of talents—the knowledge of retailing, which is the merchant's forte; the marketing director's expertise for developing and implementing traffic-building devices and coor-

---

SUGGESTED LEASE CLAUSE

Promotion and Advertising Fund

Landlord will immediately establish a Promotion and Advertising Service for the shopping center. Tenant agrees to pay Landlord — ¢ per square foot, multiplied by the gross area, payable in advance on the first day of each month, as Tenant's contribution toward the promotion, advertising, public relations, and administrative expenses related thereto. The above assessed Promotional Charge, payable by Tenant to Landlord, will be subject to adjustment commencing with the beginning of the second calendar year after lease commencement date, and each second calendar year thereafter.

Assessment shall be increased or decreased, with the adjustment to be determined as follows: use the Consumer Price Index, U.S. Average for Urban Wage Earners and Clerical Workers, All Items: 1967 = 100, published by the Bureau of Labor Statistics of the United States Department of Labor. If the Bureau of Labor Statistics changes the base period, those index numbers shall be substituted for the original ones in making the computation. If such Consumer Price Index of the United States Bureau of Labor Statistics is discontinued, comparable statistics on the purchase power of the consumer dollar shall be used for making such computation.

If Tenant shall open or be required under the terms of this lease to open for business in the Demised Premises at any time before or within ninety (90) days after the date of the Grand Opening of the Shopping Center, Tenant also agrees to pay to Landlord, in addition to the foregoing Promotion and Advertising Charge, an initial contribution in the same — ¢ per square foot amount (above) for the purpose of promotion, advertising, and public relations expenses expended by Landlord as related to the preopening and Grand Opening promotion of the Shopping Center. Such Grand Opening charge shall be paid to Landlord by Tenant within ten (10) days following the presentation of a bill to Tenant therefore, but not later than thirty (30) days before Tenant opens for business in the Demised Premises.

Furthermore, Tenant also agrees to advertise in special Shopping Center newspaper sections or tabloids sponsored by Landlord for advertising by merchants of the Shopping Center. Tenant agrees to participate in a minimum of, but not limited to, four (4) issues during each lease year. Tenant also agrees to purchase in each instance advertising space in the following minimum amounts: tabloid special sections ¼ page; 8-column sections ⅛ page. If Tenant shall refuse or neglect to submit its copy of such advertising in a timely manner, Landlord, at its election, shall have the right (but not the obligation) to submit copy consisting of Tenant's Trade Name and address to the printer for inclusion in such printed advertising media on behalf of and for the account of Tenant. If Tenant shall refuse or neglect to pay for such advertising, Landlord may pay such sums, and in such event, Tenant agrees to reimburse Landlord upon demand, and all such sums so expended shall be deemed as additional rent.

Landlord agrees to contribute not less than twenty-five (25%) percent of the total amount of the Promotion-Advertising Fund contributed by Tenants of the Shopping Center. However, Landlord, at its option, may elect to contribute all or part of the services of a Marketing Director and/or Secretary, and their respective offices, as part of such cash contribution. The Marketing Director and/or Secretary shall be under the exclusive control and supervision of the Landlord.

dinating them with merchandise events; and the developer's ability and business acumen in creating a retailing complex. A proper mix of these talents can be most beneficial to all parties—be it in the form of a merchants association or a promotional fund.

The foregoing lease clause was presented for a reason. In today's changing world of shopping centers, the marketing director is often charged with the responsibility of enforcing lease clauses that mandate not only merchants association membership or promotion fund participation, but also participation in cooperative centerwide advertising. It is, therefore, necessary that the marketing director inform the tenants that nonparticipation is in violation of the lease. If there is a repetition of this nonparticipation, the matter should be brought to the attention of the center manager, and subsequently to the owner-developer.

To perform effectively, promotion/marketing directors should be privy to details of all leases, as these can affect their day-to-day involvement with both tenants and owner. The information would include tenants' responsibility for maintaining merchants association membership or promotion fund participation and payment of dues, their inclusion in cooperative centerwide promotions, and payments of their share for center security arrangements where this is a marketing director's responsibility. Complete knowledge of these factors is important if the promotion unit is to enforce any of these lease terms. It should be clear that as the responsibilities of marketing directors have increased, their involvement in the marketing scene has grown, and will continue to grow. As defined by the American Marketing Association, marketing is "the performance of activities directed toward the flow of goods and services from producer to consumer or user." This surely sums up the new role of Promotion/Marketing Directors.

Discussion Questions 1

1. Your developer has announced plans for a new shopping center and asked for your recommendation on a merchants association or a promotion fund. Cite the pros and cons of each and develop your recommendation for either.

2. As a marketing/promotion director what clauses in a lease agreement most affect your ability to perform? Why?

3. Develop a planning timetable for a Grand Opening, outlining key steps in organizing and implementing it.

4. Describe the rationale for assessing tenants on a per-square-foot basis to support a promotional effort. What are the advantages to merchants? To the developer?

5. In a formal merchants association, what are the key committees? And why?

6. Most new shopping centers plan the preopening, Grand Opening and first year's promotional program as a continuing effort. Why? How does this affect the center's role in the marketplace?

7. Why are shopping centers analagous to vertical department stores? From a merchandising viewpoint? From the standpoint of advertising and sales promotion?

8. What posture should the shopping center marketing/promotion director take vis-à-vis the role of department stores in a center's promotion effort?

2

MARKETING TECHNIQUES

The greatest growth in the shopping center industry occurred during the late 1960s and early to middle 1970s. New centers were larger and more complicated than earlier centers. They often were constructed in proximity to existing centers and aimed at the same shopper audience. In some instances, the location of a new center or centers resulted in an enlargement of the original market area; that is, customers were drawn to the larger marketplace from a wider radius and, hence, sales potential existed for both the new and old centers. On occasion, however, the reverse occurred—the existing center suffered a loss of shoppers, volume, and prestige as a result of the new center.

The point here is not to provide a treatise on shopping center location strategy; determining locations is the province of developers, retailers, economists, and market researchers. Instead, it is to emphasize to marketing directors a fact that may be clearly defined or never stated—each shopping center does in fact have a measurable market to tap. It is within that boundary—sometimes geographic, often economic—that a center can expect to draw the maximum number of customers.

Another truism is that appointment to the role of handling a center's marketing/promotion carries with it the implied responsibility of knowing what the market is and shaping the center's posture to develop and maintain customer traffic that can be translated into an end-product—customer purchases. In brief, that is what shopping center marketing is all about.

The essential tool in this all-important task is market research. Actually, extensive market research and analysis was undertaken long before a decision was made to build. In many instances, studies were conducted periodically to keep abreast of changing market conditions. This initial and ongoing market analysis was vital for the developer. It delivered information that enabled the developer to lease to retailers who will provide the best tenant "mix" for the area. The research data revealed facts such as population in numbers, age dominance and/or mix, income range, shopping preference, home ownership and average cost, and ethnic composition. These data were applied by the owner to achieve a balance of tenants that will best serve the needs of the center's shopping community.

Lessees (tenants) similarly benefited from market surveys—their own as well as the developer's. The initial survey provided information that enabled retailers to merchandise and stock their stores based on "hard" facts rather than "feel." Ongoing analysis also provides the checks and balances necessary to keep current in a market characterized by changes in life styles, economic factors, population density, ethnic makeup, shopping habits, and so on.

Such research and subsequent analysis also delivers both the demographics and psychographics necessary to keep pace in the fast-moving, ever-changing retailing world. The information provides direction and substance to the positioning of the center within its primary and secondary market areas.

"Positioning" is a relatively new word in shopping center terminology, and is used in describing the many and diverse methods of marketing a center. Simply defined, it is the intelligent use of every segment of marketing, merchandising, promotion, publicity, public relations, special events, and so forth, on an interrelated, ongoing basis, to establish recognition of the center and give it a strong positive identity in the minds of consumers.

To position properly requires periodic research and analysis and use of the material as a road map to keep the center on course toward the defined objective. A changing market, as perceived by analysis, may mean a detour from the original plan, and therein lies the importance and value of research on a recurring basis.

For the professional marketing director, it is essential to have the following information for guidance in positioning a center in its markets. This information is vital for the director establishing a center's first marketing plan as well as for his or her efforts in existing centers.

• A study of the primary and secondary market area, that is, estimated driving time and distance, major and alternate routes, population density in the primary and secondary markets, and possible peripheral areas that can be exploited profitably.

• Demographics of the consumer, including median age and income, ownership and value of homes, education level, employment categories, sex of respondents, attitudes about existing regional shopping centers, including likes, dislikes, and frequency of visits, as well as awareness of the proposed center.

• Facts about the center: number and types of stores (merchandise categories, chains and independents) now open, including anchor stores by name, number of stores in center when center is complete, condition of access roads to the center, and condition of parking lots in the center.

• Analysis of competition: number of regional and/or smaller centers in the primary and secondary market areas, proximity to your center, number of stores, anchors by name, enclosed or open malls, image, consumer demographics. Separate lists for primary and secondary market areas.

Much of this is available during the building/leasing stages to guide the developer in the leasing process and provide direction for the retailers in merchandising their stores. Such data can provide facts that will enable tenants to segment their customer audience, select fast-moving merchandise with reasonable accuracy, and adjust their price points to the economic levels of potential shoppers.

To ensure strong positioning of the center in its primary and secondary markets, the trade areas should be the subject of ongoing research and analysis, as a check on current direction and a test of the accuracy of the original research, as soon as is practical after the center opening. The information revealed by these surveys can be applied to a variety of promotion and marketing plans, and forms the basis of an overall marketing strategy. Among the promotion/marketing elements affected are:

• Merchandise promotion—review the calendar of events, especially the types of promotion (sales, clearance, institutional, image building) in light of shopper preferences revealed in the market analysis. Also, the plans for on-the-mall sales events (i.e. sidewalk, moonlite, midnite sales).

• Traffic-building devices—the supplements to merchandise promotions, and those used in the building of shopping awareness of the center.

• Media—segmentations, buying, and placement—vital factors in the process of strongly positioning a mall in its markets.

• Image building—defining by the printed word (newspapers and circulars) as well as television and radio (the electronic media) what the center represents: more value, more choice, more courtesy, more shopping convenience and comfort. It also relates to the format for the print media, and the musical jingle and signature for television and radio that was created to "trigger" instant recognition.

• Community relations—ascertaining what the community seeks and creating a feeling that the shopping center is an integral part of the local scene. Community leaders should be asked to suggest activities that would be most beneficial, and the center should review the suggestions, implementing as many as the budget will allow, provided they are truly community-oriented and will add to the reservoir of good will.

Having segmented the markets and digested pertinent information, it is now the responsibility of the marketing director to develop plans and programs. Sharing this information among tenants for their use in determining their own merchandising strategies is an important by-product of the research process. It is only through this fact-finding that an effective promotion-advertising-publicity-public relations program can be set into motion. Today's competitive climate virtually mandates this kind of effort in order to establish and maintain the position of the center in the primary and secondary market areas, and its environs.

With the increase in sophistication of marketing plans for centers, the responsibilities and contributions of marketing-promotion directors to the success of their center has also increased. Their role has undergone significant change in recent years, and there is far more than semantical significance in the change in title from "Promotion" to "Marketing Director."

In the earliest days of trial and error, testing, then retention or discard, promotion directors laboriously built a roster of events, both merchandise and nonmerchandise. When this cycle ended, they were ready to move into the next phase, which included budget preparation, the scheduling of events, coordinating merchandise promotions with customer traffic-building devices, and delivering this information to tenants clearly and in time to take the necessary action. Perhaps the most important duty of the marketing director today is to establish a clear, positive image of the center—an image that is in keeping with the center's own individual market.

Creating customer traffic for the shopping center has always been and continues to be one of the major jobs of the marketing director. In the past, the role was to "deliver the bodies" to the center, and from that point on individual merchants took over by participating in the events actively, passively, or not at all. The results usually were in relation to their efforts: good, bad, or indifferent. Experience demonstrates that we cannot "stand pat" on the breadth, scope, and content of center-wide promotion as it has evolved thus far. We must build on the basics that have been developed through past experience and trial and error. The knowledge of past successes and failures has presented promotion/marketing directors with an opportunity to diversify and to expand their activities into phases of marketing, an important related area, as developers rely more heavily on market research.

Marketing directors rarely conduct the preopening surveys, but they can contribute to, or sometimes take over part of the survey process as a regular part of their responsibilities after the center's opening. In any case, they should be familiar with survey results and implications and provide merchants with a profile of their market each time a survey has been completed.

The fact-gathering process, while not difficult, can be time-consuming and technical. Much of the information is readily available from "free" sources—government agencies, banks, utilities, media, chambers of commerce, and the like. Often, anchor stores or smaller tenants in the center will share selected data they have amassed. Spot checks of license plates, customer interviews, and the like can relate this directly to the center under study. Professional researchers can be engaged to perform the service. Centers can use their own staff, or enlist college and high school students, to undertake the fact-gathering. But it is the marketing director—charged with developing and implementing a total "positioning" program—who must take the initiative to gather facts, analyze them, and find the appropriate "handles."

15

What follows are two sample questionnaires. They address the questions to be asked, although obviously in outline form; the questions should be tailored to the needs of individual shopping centers. The first questionnaire relates to consumer awareness, shopping patterns, identifications, and so forth, and is designed as a preopening telephone study, to be completed in time for use during the leasing process. The second is a consumer survey study, conducted on the mall, not later than two months after the opening of a center.

Bel Air Shopping City Questionnaire

Preopening Telephone Survey
Random Selection of Respondents from Primary and Secondary Market Areas

Introduction:
Good morning, (afternoon - evening). This is _____ representing Williams Research Consultants. We are calling on behalf of Bel Air Mall, which is opening soon in Asheville, and gathering information for a study of the shopping habits of you and your neighbors, so we can serve you better. Are you (may I) speak to the lady of the house?

Thank you; I promise to be brief;

1. Awareness of Area Shopping Centers
Ask respondents which mall they visit most often? Second choice? Third choice? Any others? Which are *not* enclosed malls?

2. Shopping Patterns
Last mall visit? Mall name? Other malls (names) visited in past 3 months? How many visits to all malls? How many were *not* enclosed? Mall visited most often? Why do you prefer (mall name) to others in area? (Ask specific questions about reasons for preference until answers become illogical) Drive time (from home/business) to preferred and other malls?

3. Bel Air Shopping City Research
Ask respondents if they know about Bel Air Mall: Its location at N.C. Highway 280, Exit 9? Planned opening date? Number of stores, including anchors? (Give this information as most will not have these details unless the publicity campaign is in high gear) Plans to visit Bel Air? How often? Travel by private car? Bus? Travel time from home? Business? Know best routes?

4. Miscellaneous
Charge cards at any of anchor stores? Visa? Master Charge? American Express? Employment (lady of house) outside of home? Full time? Part time? Age? Education? Total household income? Newspapers read daily? TV and radio stations most favored? Second choice? Third choice?

Bel Air Shopping City

Mall Consumer Survey Questionnaire

1. General Information
Date; day of week; time of day; sex of respondent.

2. Address and Bel Air Accessibility
Street and number? City, state, zip code? Distance (miles) to shopping center from home? Distance (miles) to shopping center from business? Elapsed time: from home? from business?

3. Shopping Patterns
How often does respondent visit Bel Air? How often does respondent visit other centers? If Bel Air visits more frequent, give reasons. If other centers more frequently shopped, give names and reasons. What 3 days of week (in order of preference) does respondent shop? What hours are *most* preferred? What days and hours are *least* preferred? Does respondent shop alone? With family, friends, relatives? Average purchases (dollars) on each visit? Payment by cash, credit card, charge?

4. Personal Statistics (demographics)
Age? Marital status? Level of education? Own home or rent? How many reside in home? Market value of home if owned? Children in home? Ages of children? Employment of adults? Full time? Part time? Total annual income of occupants? Which newspapers does respondent read daily? What 3 radio stations are preferred? What times are they most listened to? What 3 TV stations are preferred? What categories (sports, weather, news, comedy, drama) are viewed most frequently? Is daytime or nighttime TV favored?

5. Summary
Is the attitude of store personnel in Bel Air warm and courteous? Would this influence frequent visits? Is the mall clean and an inviting place for shopping? Was there sufficient parking space during your last 3 visits? Were the lots well illuminated if your visit was after dark? What facilities, services or improvements would you suggest to make Bel Air Shopping City an even better shopping experience?

These samples may be used during the pre- and postopening periods. With revisions resulting from timing and locale, they can be adapted for recurring analysis and focus group interviews, which are a part of the ongoing research program in some centers.

While modern methods of evaluating and positioning shopping centers in their correct segment of the marketplace are used by large developers, these techniques are by no means limited to them. Smaller centers, as well, as would do well to reexamine their policies and programs to make certain they are aimed at the right consumer audience, and redirect their efforts to reach and maintain the most profitable market position, where they are not.

Two other vital parts of the research process are an analysis of the competition, from both marketing and sales perspectives, and an analysis of your own center's sales patterns.

If a marketing director is to properly position the center in the marketplace, he or she must be intimately acquainted with the strengths and weaknesses of competing centers or retail districts in the area. He or she must know the kinds of shops other centers have, the segment of the market to which these centers appeal, the nature of their advertising and promotional efforts, physical assets and liabilities, approximate sales volumes, and overall image in the market. The marketing strategy later developed for Bel Air Center will reflect this information. The marketing director will work to capitalize on the weaknesses of the other centers in the area.

A knowledge of your own center's sales patterns, as well as retail sales patterns in general, can help you analyze how your center is performing in relation to retail trends as a whole, and from year to year within the center itself. In addition, this information can help you determine which product lines should be bolstered by promotions, and when these promotions should be held.

Effective market research can give the marketing director the sharp knife needed to carve out a large slice of a competitive market. Demographic data and survey results provide a picture of the trade area from which the center's sales will come. Advertising and special events can be planned and targeted to a specific audience. The physical boundaries established through research can help when planning a media mix. Finally, understanding of the competition further helps the marketing director find a position for the center not only in the overall market, but also in relation to the other centers in overlapping markets.

Discussion Questions 2

1. How do market conditions today differ from the early days of shopping centers? Why?

2. Has the role of market research for new shopping centers changed over the years? Is it more or less important? Why?

3. Aside from justifying a decision on location, what other benefits of market research accrue to a developer? To a merchant?

4. What is meant by "positioning" a center in a marketplace? What are the key steps in measuring the center's "position"?

5. Discuss briefly the key ingredients in establishing a center's proper "position" in its trade area.

6. Who is responsible for the marketing strategy of a shopping center? Why?

7. How does one measure the impact of competition on a shopping center? What crucial information must be obtained?

8. Discuss the kinds of information a marketing director should have about the center's customers and would-be customers. Outline the sources for such information.

3

PREOPENING PUBLICITY

In the promotion of a new shopping center, an expansion, or a renovation, the preopening publicity is the first phase that the public is aware of. Ideally, it should begin six to twelve months prior to the opening. For a new center, the goal is to begin building the center's "image," to establish its location, and to identify its role within the community. With expansion or renovation, the goal is to enhance the center's competitive edge in the market. In both cases, the approach is usually "soft sell," with emphasis on newsworthy stories ("topping," design, plans, progress) and personal interviews (key center personnel, local store owners moving to the center, and the like).

The preopening publicity is vital in setting the stage for what is to come. It is counterproductive to neglect or delay publicity because emphasis is placed on completing construction of the center by the target date. Too often a publicity effort begun only a month or so before opening requires a crash effort that can be expensive, suffer from loss of free publicity which would have been derived over a longer period of time, and must be supplemented with expensive print ads, television, and radio. In addition, the image-building, location-identification, and community-participation process accomplished over a span of many months is difficult to match in a few short weeks.

The preopening publicity plan is the least complex of the many facets of shopping center promotion. The amount of publicity received and the effectiveness of the effort depends on three equally important factors:

• The budget
• The agency or individual handling the preopening publicity
• The campaign plan

As stated earlier, the expense for preopening promotion for a new center is usually handled as part of an initial assessment charged to shopping center tenants and the developer. If preopening promotion funds are still inadequate, the department stores and developer will frequently share the deficit rather than curtail the opening promotion. The publicity portion of the preopening is relatively inexpensive—covering releases, photos, printing, mailing, possibly business luncheons and press functions.

THE PROFESSIONAL HANDLING PREOPENING PUBLICITY

The promotion work is usually executed by a professional who has the expertise to get the most mileage out of every available dollar and to derive the maximum benefits from stories in the press and other news media. This expert can be chosen from an agency well versed in publicity and public relations or from the publicity staff of the developer's home office. Alternatively, the individual who will eventually handle the center's promotion once it is fully operational may be responsible for the campaign.

About six months before opening or reopening (or just as the merchants association is to come into being for a new center) is usually the best time to launch the preopening publicity phase. Tenants, particularly the department stores, should be consulted, not only to keep them informed but as a way to develop newsworthy stories.

Early in the campaign, the emphasis is on sheer publicity—(news), but, as the opening approaches, the emphasis shifts to a combination of news and promotion—events—because the effort to position the center within its market begins to heighten.

The merchants association bylaws will usually stipulate whether the developer, the merchants association membership, or its board of directors has the power of decision, but it falls upon the marketing director or agency to function on an operational basis and implement basic decisions reached. From a practical point of view it is usually the developer who has the most say in the preopening program.

THE CAMPAIGN PLAN

The early stages of preopening publicity can be handled effectively, and with little or no cost, by well-placed, well-timed releases to newspapers in the prime and secondary trading areas and through the building, on a casual basis, of contacts in the local media. Here are some possible stories, which can be applied to an expansion or renovation as well as a new center.

- **The Tenants.** Include their business and personal background, their merchandise mix, price lines, services offered, special features that will be available in the new stores, and so forth. Local merchants and department store representatives can be interviewed, and the home offices of chain-store tenants can provide all information necessary for the stories. The news releases should particularly emphasize the employment of members of the community plus the subsequent economic benefit to the area, as well as the personalized service shoppers will receive.

- **The Merchant Mix.** Give the range of merchandise and services offered by the center, an enumeration of the various items that may be purchased, and the services that can be performed. Stress the "something for everyone" concept and the availability of merchandise from popular priced to designer goods.

- **The Exact Location.** Identify the specific roads or highways that encircle the center. Also, the distance in miles or driving time from all familiar points in the trading area.

- **The Area in Terms of Acreage.** Describe the area occupied by the entire shopping center complex, including all buildings and the parking lots.

- **The Space in Square Feet.** Give the exact area occupied by tenants offering both merchandise and services, but particularly the anchor stores, which should receive the benefit of as much publicity as possible.

- **The Parking Area.** Include the number of cars that can be accommodated, the ease of access from parking lots to the stores, and any pertinent details such as well-illuminated lots and security measures, which are important to evening shoppers, especially.

- **Unusual Construction Features.** Describe any all-weather, climate-controlled features that are very important to today's shoppers and to publicity. (Climate-controlled malls are more comfortable than the older open malls). Also mention the type of architecture (particularly if it blends into local design), the construction and design features in individual stores.

- **The Architects.** Identify the individual architects, their role in the industry (from the strip centers of the early years to the present multilevel, all-weather, climate-controlled centers), current design approaches, and other newsworthy details. Similar publicity can be developed for interior designers, landscape experts, and other professionals involved in the design of the center.

- **The Builders.** Report on the people who actually built the center—often they are from the area and known to residents. This factor, together with the employment of local craftsmen, should be fully exploited to heighten interest in the center among local residents. Stories should also be developed around subcontractors responsible for heating, air conditioning, electrical work, and carpentry, most of whom also will be local or area residents. This will further link the upcoming shopping center with the community and help create a very desirable image.

- **The Owner-Developer.** Reveal pertinent details about the key professional in charge. Whether the developer is a real estate specialist with experience in shopping center development or an entrepreneur with multifaceted activities, the public will want to know more about who is building the center. If the developer has opened other centers in the area, the new project will generate more than usual interest. If this is the first for the locality, stories on contributions made by centers in other areas can be helpful in building up attention within the market area.

- **The Image.** Include the business and philanthropic endeavors of the developer. If the developer is an area resident, stress this in news releases to engender good will at the outset and help identify the project with the betterment of the community.

- **Additional Story Subjects.** Publicize the new developments on the local scene that are the result of the center. Describe the new or improved roads providing access to the center, include statements on the involvement in community affairs, and announce events related to the center's management personnel—all are timely topics for the community.

Four to six weeks before the center opens, the preopening effort should shift from the low-key editorial approach to one with increasing impact. At this point, too, the program should begin to accelerate and funds allocated in the preopening budget should be spent for a series of promotional newspaper ads, and, depending on the budget and market, special radio and TV spots. Where available, zoned editions of newspapers are best, permitting ads to be targeted to reach the maximum audience of potential shoppers in the prime and secondary market areas where they are needed most, and at a lower cost than would have been incurred for a full-run ad.

The preopening budget may also call for roadside billboards located at as many access points to the center as possible. The billboards must stress the opening date, pinpoint the location, state the number of stores and services, and name the anchor stores. Although the mention of anchor stores may appear to be favored treatment and could cause other merchants to object, the big stores generally "pull" much of the customer traffic and most likely will be consistent advertisers during the preopening and postopening periods.

Use of television spots, their frequency and type, will be dictated by the budget. Television is an effective promotional tool, but it is the most expensive of the media. Furthermore, it is not possible to buy zoned spots aimed at the prime and secondary markets only; thus, a substantial number of the viewers may not be potential shoppers. Although a similar situation exists in the use of radio, that medium has the great added advantage of reaching customers when they are in their automobiles. As a result, radio can attract shoppers from outside the immediate market area where television usually does not. Jingles—catchy, engaging musical renditions—are invaluable, and should be developed and repeated, again and again, as another vehicle for instant center identification.

The campaign should be informative, positive, and attention-getting. It should increase in intensity and scope as the opening approaches and reach its peak during the three days immediately preceding the opening. At that point, every medium being used should be working on a saturation basis, vividly telling the story of the center. Details of the opening celebration should unfold progressively during the period, to be summarized again and again during the several days preceding the center's opening.

The important items to be stressed all during this phase, with a sharp increase in stress just prior to the opening are:

- The center's opening date.

- The exact location of the center and its accessibility to all sections of the trading area. Detailed maps in the print media and specified routes to the center on the radio and on television spots will help in this.

- A tenant listing together with merchandise or services offered.

- The opening and closing hours of the center's tenants, with particular emphasis on the closing hour because shopping centers traditionally are most heavily trafficked during the evening.

- The free parking facilities, the number of cars the lot will accommodate, and the ease and convenience of parking.

Discussion Questions 3

1. If a center has many months before it opens, what advantages are there to an extensive preopening publicity effort?

2. What factors should be taken into account in planning and conducting a preopening or reopening publicity program?

3. What news will local media be most interested in about a new center or a renovation? Why?

4. Outline a program to develop newsworthy information about a new center or renovation, listing kinds of news and likely sources.

5. Larger stores usually capture greater attention from local news media. Develop a program to publicize smaller stores.

6. Aside from print, radio, and television, what other media are available to marketing directors publicizing a new or renovated center? Cite their value.

4

GRAND OPENING PROMOTION

After months and years of planning, building, organizing, publicizing, and promoting, a dream that was just a gleam in the developer's eye is about to become a reality. From countless meetings with architects, builders, bankers, leasing agents, and potential tenants there has emerged a shopping center, ready to serve the surrounding market area and ready to become an integral part of its community.

Because first impressions are usually lasting, the Grand Opening or Grand Reopening promotion must be well planned, must have the support of the anchor stores, chains, and local merchants, and it must be adequately funded. If promotion is to be effective, the elements that follow, which form the nucleus of any shopping center's promotional activity, must be strongly exploited by every possible means and in every possible medium.

Before examining the details of the actual Grand Opening promotion, however, it would be helpful to review the practical logistics that lead to the Grand Opening.

OPERATION GRAND OPENING

The mechanics and logistics of the grand opening or reopening must be planned in great detail at least six months in advance and carried out with precision. The hallmark of a smooth professional opening is that the myriad related details are scheduled and completed in the proper sequence and on time.

Usually one member of the owner-management team—a director of operations, or whatever the title—is responsible for, and the motivating force behind, the planning and implementation of an opening program. This includes laying out the timetable, developing the responsibility lists (the means whereby the various details are assigned to staff members) and delegating specific duties and functions to the center manager and the marketing/promotion director and/or agency.

As a case in point, our mythical center, Bel Air Shopping City, was scheduled to open October 5. A general outline of the Grand Opening Plan was developed early during the preceding April. At that point, the plan was necessarily tentative and general, but it included an estimate of the budget for the Grand Opening period; a survey of the prime and secondary market areas to be serviced by the center; a review of available media, both print and electronic, as well as billboard locations; and interviews with available advertising-promotion agencies or individuals, as well as candidates for the job of mail manager and marketing director.

Necessary preliminaries to the next step—the development of a more detailed program—included the following specifics: media to be used, as determined by a market-area survey; investigation, then decision, on the locations of the billboards to announce the center's opening; and, of course, the hiring of the mall manager and of the promotion/marketing director.

Then, approximately five months before the opening, further elements of the general plan were laid out and developed in great detail on the "Responsibility Lists." They became the "Bible" of those responsible for the smooth, punctual, successful opening that took place.

A part of Appendix A is the highly detailed "Responsibility List" that was drawn up for preparation of the Bel Air Shopping City opening. It is, of course, adaptable to every other center opening.

Also included with Appendix A is a Bel Air Shopping City "Countdown," which supplements the Responsibility List by highlighting exceptionally important dates and events. This was distributed to personnel well in advance of the first scheduled date, and responsibility for its implementation was assigned to various members of the Bel Air Shopping City team.

Depending on the extent of preparation required for the items on the countdown, and the experience of the staff handling their implementation, it might be advisable to ask the staff to supply a sequential listing of the steps necessary to accomplish their assignments.

MERCHANDISE PROMOTION

The most important element of a Grand Opening is the merchandise promotion. A necessary part of this promotion is a coordinated advertising program.

All promotion plans should include a special section devoted to merchandise, and every merchant urged to advertise. Included in this section would be editorial material and photographs relating to the tenants, their merchandise, and their services (if any). To assure maximum participation, many leases now mandate advertising in all shopping center special sections, including the Grand Opening publication.

If there is no covering lease clause, merchants must be urged, in the strongest possible terms, to be a part of the Grand Opening special section.

As the budget permits, the special sections may be inserted in area dailies, weeklies, and any available zoned newspaper editions, and supplemented by overruns delivered to homes not covered by the local papers.

The kind of merchandising to be featured in the opening advertisements is completely the domain of the individual merchants, based on their own policy and judgment. Some stores will promote "Opening Specials," while others will run opening-announcement ads that are institutional in nature. Although the merchandising policies of various tenants within a center may be poles apart, every merchant, by presenting merchandise at regular or sale prices, adds impact and customer "pull-power" to every section published.

Since tenants are in shopping centers to sell merchandise and, equally axiomatic, the center was built as a retailing entity, it follows that the most direct route to maximum results is to merchandise as a unit. This means maximum tenant participation in advertising that can be translated into greater reader interest, resulting in greater customer traffic and, finally, greater dollar volume. The best time to take advantage of these basic retailing facts is during the Grand Opening period, when curiosity about the center and its merchants is at the highest point.

IN-CENTER TRAFFIC BUILDERS

Official ceremonies should be well-publicized and are usually scheduled to be completed by the normal opening hour; on-the-mall activities can supplement the official Grand Opening or Grand Reopening. There is the traditional ribbon-cutting ceremony, presided over by the owner-developer, a representative, or by a well-known personality. When notables and "names" from the world of politics, entertainment, or sports attend, the magnetism is heightened.

Following the opening ceremonies and continuing for several days afterward, traffic building devices should be designed to attract potential shoppers into the center. It is important, however, to keep on-the-mall activities to a reasonable level and to time them properly, because they tend to keep potential buyers on the mall and out of stores. Mall activities should take place during normally low traffic periods and end just before customer activity accelerates.

Many Grand Openings generate "wall-to-wall" customer traffic, but mediocre to disappointing sales volume results.

In these circumstances disappointing results are understandable. Some promotion directors will take issue with this point, arguing that the Grand Opening period should be used to introduce the center to the community in the most favorable conditions, and, having accomplished this, visitors will subsequently return to make the center a regular shopping habit. The retailer's view is that a successful Grand Opening period includes *both* "wall-to-wall" customer traffic and brisk sales. Both goals can be attained with the proper mix of merchandise promotion and the judicious timing of traffic-building devices. While an impressive unveiling of the center is important for future community relations, volume for the tenant and overages for the landlord are still primary.

On-the-mall events must, therefore, be designed to supplement and not overly dominate Grand Opening promotion activities. *Merchandise offerings and not spectaculars, are the reasons customers come to centers*—an object to be borne in mind at all times.

Almost everyone who visits a shopping center is a potential buyer. If the Grand Opening period is successful, they will return on future visits. The ideal Grand Opening affords the opportunity and the desire to visit the stores as well as participate in the ceremonial festivities.

Keep in mind that Grand Opening traffic is always inflated, and not a true indicator of normal attendance. Some of those visiting the center from outside the primary and secondary market areas will rarely, if ever, return. But the vast majority of those attending are potential customers who can become regular shoppers because the new center is convenient and offers a fine choice of stores, plenty of free parking, and a host of other conveniences that equal or exceed those available elsewhere. The proportion of visitors who will make the new center a regular shopping habit often is directly related to the impact of their initial visit. "Opportunity" and "desire" to shop and purchase goods are the strongest factors influencing their decisions to return, and the Grand Opening promotion is the time to set the stage.

RADIO AND TELEVISION

Both radio and television are excellent media that can be used to unfold the total shopping center story and project an image. The earlier preopening messages focused on the advantages and desirability of shopping in the center—easy accessibility, balanced merchant mix, vast merchandise selections and services, shopping comfort, ample and easy parking facilities, and store hours convenient for family shopping.

With that phase completed, effective merchandise promotion would dominate the radio and television messages during the Grand Opening period. Although print-media special sections will provide merchandise details and generate some excitement, the shopping community should be saturated with news of the opening promotion and the merchandise available through radio and television spots. Integrally combined in the spots should be descriptions of in-center traffic builders—chosen carefully and timed properly.

In this way, radio or television spots play a triple role—they tell the total shopping center story, they exploit the traffic-building devices that have been programmed, and they highlight the opening merchandise presentations of the center's merchants. Timing the spot announcements is crucial. Here is a suggested timetable that can help you schedule media announcements for the best possible results.

• Preopening announcements one week or more prior to the opening date should concentrate on the story of the shopping center. Publicized subjects should include the opening date, the exact location of the center, store hours, and merchant and merchandise mix. During this period short "teasers" can be used to signal the beginning of the opening merchandise promotion.

• Starting one week before and continuing up to three days before the Grand Opening, news of the traffic-generating devices should dominate the spots and news of the opening merchandise promotion should be accelerated. A subtle shift in emphasis from the traffic builders to merchandise promotion should occur during the last day of this period.

• Starting three days before and continuing through the Grand Opening period, all stops should be pulled on the opening merchandise promotion. The spots immediately preceding the center's Grand Opening should promote merchandise with great frequency and in the strongest possible terms. These would, of course, be supplemented by a limited number of announcements about the in-center traffic builders, as well as store hours, location, and so forth.

Television spots are expensive to produce and time costs are high. Many centers budget much of their electronic expenditures for radio and use television for times of maximum impact. Package deals offered by radio and television stations often are attractive and offer considerable cost-saving factors. In addition, the availability of a common rate for stores and the merchants association generally can stimulate merchant participation, and thus effect greater exposure for a center.

Discussion Questions 4

1. Aside from the ability to plan and communicate, what other skills must a marketing director bring to conducting a Grand Opening?

2. In what ways does a Grand Opening affect the future of a new center or a renovation?

3. What is more important for a Grand Opening—traffic or sales volume? Give reasons.

4. What types of on-the-mall events work best for Grand Openings?

5. What factors influence Grand Opening shoppers to make a new center a "shopping habit"?

6. How does one measure the success of a Grand Opening?

7. What lessons can be learned from this event?

5

PROMOTING THE CENTER AS A UNIT

Every plan or action by the merchants association, as it relates to promotion, must recognize the necessity for cooperative effort. There has been much discussion, controversy, and even dissension about this all-important principle, and it is frequently the cause of a split into factions within merchants associations.

In the ideal shopping center, all stores will be promoted as a single cohesive unit, and not as individual components. Since unity is essential, an important function of the promotion/marketing director is to foster cohesion and cooperation.

As in most groups or committees, within every shopping center there are to be found three distinct groups: "the cooperators," "the middle-of-the-roaders," and "the dissenters." While, in theory, these divisions should not exist if tenants are required, by lease, to participate in merchants association or promotion fund sponsored events, they do exist much too frequently.

● **The Cooperators.** Those who realize the vital importance of unanimity of purpose and action by the center merchants. Active within the association, they will freely express their objections if they feel a proposed action or promotion would not benefit the center. However, even if the project is approved over their objections they will honestly support it. They provide a necessary balance in most associations and often act as the liaison between the other two merchant factions. Unfortunately, they are much too often in the minority.

● **The Middle-of-the-Roaders.** Usually the majority, they will cooperate with a promotional effort if it coincides with their own plans, but will not support programs that do not. Many reasons will be advanced for their nonparticipation: lack of budget, methods contrary to policy or principles, poor timing, and so on. In general, the main reason for their nonparticipation is disinterest in the specific promotion because they disagree with the approach or concept. Since the largest number of merchants are in this category, this is the group to use as a sounding board and to approach with compromise plans. A compromise that does not drastically change the original concept or timing is far preferable to no promotion at all or to promotion that is weakened by nonparticipation of major center merchants.

● **The Dissenters.** Usually equal in size to the cooperators, but not identified with them by any other characteristics, the dissenters generally disassociate themselves from center-wide promotional activity. Disinterest, apathy, expense, and genuine disagreement with the importance of promoting a shopping center as a single unit are the most frequent reasons given for nonparticipation. The dissenters believe that merchants can and should produce their own traffic and consistently develop their own promotional approach as an entity separate from their colleagues.

When the dissenting group includes major stores, their effect is to seriously dilute any unified, centerwide promotional effort. If only a small minority, their nonparticipation usually is far more harmful to their own sales volume than to the center as a whole.

DEALING WITH STORE MANAGERS

Where factions and dissension exist, every effort must be made to gain the full support of all tenants for the promotion and publicity programs. In doing this, the marketing director must be at his or her political best—posing convincing arguments, developing meaningful programs, persuading and cajoling. If cooperation cannot be gained at the local level, chain-store home officers must be contacted and persuaded. Developers, managers, and key tenants must support the director's efforts. There are no rules or guidelines that can be applied to produce maximum cooperation, so factionalism is always a serious problem. In fact, the difficulties caused by dissension have contributed to the formation of promotion funds, solely controlled by the developer through the marketing director.

MERCHANT PARTICIPATION

A majority of center merchants, including the anchor stores, must be a part of every cooperative merchandise promotion if it is to be productive and to attain the maximum goals.

To achieve an exciting, productive merchandise section, the promotion director or agency must sell the idea of participation to the tenants. Written memoranda and/or telephone conversations are the first logical step. But experience proves that securing the cooperation required for a strong representative section makes mandatory the next step— personal contact with merchants. If participation cannot be attained at the local level, a tactful telephone call or a letter to a home office may be necessary. While the home offices may not always overrule their local representative on participation, there is always the chance that the matter may not have been discussed previously or was not properly presented by the local representative. Under any circumstances, the stage may have been set for future participation once the home office has been advised of a problem. Always remember, however, that you must deal with the local manager on a daily basis, so diplomacy is vital if you decide to contact the home office.

The approach to independent local merchants must be lower-key and softer-sell. Again

person-to-person discussions are advisable if memoranda and/or telephone calls fail in their objective. Usually the owner, not the manager, will ultimately make the decision on participation. Although local merchants do not generally comprise a majority of the tenant population in a shopping center, their participation should be actively sought because of their close identity with the community.

In most new centers, participation in merchandise promotions often is mandated by lease. Many older centers that do not have such lease clauses, achieve the same degree of participation through a contract or agreement between the merchants association and the stores.

By vote of the board of directors or the general membership, the marketing director (or agency) is instructed to prepare a program of cooperative merchandise advertising, subject to their approval. Next, space allocations are made to individual merchants based on their occupied gross area or volume. Contracts (and a covering letter of explanation) are then prepared for merchant-tenant approval. Every effort is made to secure approval for an entire year so there will be no lapse in the continuity. If this fails, a six-month or thirteen-week contract is better than none at all. While this approach is intended for newspaper ads, much the same technique can be used for joint radio and television commercials.

Two methods of payment are used for a contracted merchant-participation plan. It is usually best to increase merchant association dues to cover the entire cost of the program, because most leases and merchant association bylaws permit dues increases by a majority vote or a two-thirds vote of the general membership. However, some centers have developed and implemented advertising programs without an increase in merchants association dues, which means payment for individual ads by individual tenants. Given a choice, a dues increase that includes the cost of all advertising is far preferable, because it assures participation or a merchant's loss of prepaid ad space.

A typical annual contract, together with its covering letter, that includes the cost of advertising space is part of Appendix D. It can be used as is, or adapted for a six-month or thirteen-week period. Such documents should be given to both local management and home offices. This distribution will assure a fair evaluation of the program and will accelerate a decision.

Timing of Merchandise Promotions

The timing of promotions is usually determined by the board of directors in conjunction with the marketing director (or agency). The schedule is then approved by the general membership, and disseminated to center store managers, to chain-store home offices, and to department-store parent offices. The program covers an entire upcoming year and is developed, approved, and distributed well in advance of the first promotion. If the center is operating with a promotion fund, the marketing director (or developer representative) develops the program and may review it with a merchant steering committee (this review is optional, not mandatory).

A sample first-year budget and promotion program is provided in Appendix C. A program of this nature should be fully operative upon completion of the Grand Opening period (which continues for at least 30 days after the center opening). Promotions and budgets for subsequent years should also be planned in advance, to allow a sufficient period, prior to the first scheduled cooperative merchandise promotion, in which to contact and persuade merchants to join in the effort.

Advance planning is vital in order to maintain a close liaison with the anchors, particularly if they are part of a department store group. It is, of course, an established fact that department stores project promotion and advertising expenditures for six months to a year ahead. It is also incontestable that their ongoing advertising and promotion generates substantial center traffic, which works to the benefit of all merchants. It is important, therefore, that department store promotions be coordinated not only with other branches in the area but with the individual centers in which they are located.

For the center's marketing director (or agency) this means developing the advertising and promotion program to coordinate, as nearly as possible, with the events scheduled by the anchor stores. Because different dates for promotions are inevitable, compromises will be necessary to secure consistent participation from the majors.

Many chain stores and local merchants will, inevitably, complain about and, indeed, resent the coordination of cooperative merchandise promotions with anchor store events. However, anchor store participation is crucial and accommodation is essential to overall success.

Notifying the Merchants

Although each merchant, and each home office where applicable, will have received a copy of the projected six-month or one-year promotional program and budget, it is essential to renotify them about each promotion well in advance of each deadline. The information should be provided as a separate communication, with no other subject or item included. If the basic plan is sent together with the minutes of a merchants association meeting or in a bulletin with assorted other subjects, the essential ingredients may be overlooked.

A single sheet that delivers all the facts in a timely manner is the most effective reminder. Appendix D contains a sample fact sheet and, when completed, it will provide tenants all the facts relating to an upcoming merchandise promotion. Timing is important; the fact sheet should reach all tenants at least five weeks prior to deadline dates. This allows sufficient time for chain and department stores to contact home offices and parent stores for authorization to participate and for the preparation of the advertisements, merchandise, display material, and instructions.

In many instances poor or inadequate participation in planned centerwide promotions can be traced to late receipt of a communication about the event, or to missing details that were essential to preparation. Nonparticipation is rarely the result of an established policy of noncooperation. However, poor timing and incomplete details provide ready excuses for store managers, particularly if they must receive authorization to advertise from their home offices. The marketing director must recognize that participation is not limited to the creation of an advertisement, but involves merchandising and timing. For example, buyers must coordinate plans in one store with the rest of a chain- or department-store group. Their plans may involve production of appropriate display material, instructions to the store managers on pricing, markdown procedures, and window and interior display of the advertised items.

The most important aspect of the promotional "handle" is that it be related to the position the center wishes to achieve in the market. For example, if research reveals that the center's customers are predominantly young families, the merchandise specials and corresponding promotional events must be keyed to this group.

STORE HOURS
One of the least understood and yet most important aspects of shopping center unanimity is the establishment and observance of uniform store hours. Opening and closing hours are usually stipulated by lease after consultation with the anchor stores, or are determined and voted upon at the merchants association organizational meeting. In the latter instance, the anchor stores are the determining factors in establishing the opening and closing schedules, as they should be.

Once the matter has been settled, all stores, large and small, must adhere to both the opening and closing hours that have been agreed on. Unanimity enables the center merchants to operate as an entity rather than as individuals; it provides authenticity for advertising that mentions center hours and, above all, prevents disappointment to shoppers who come to the center to visit specific stores, only to find them closed.

Merchants who do not follow the official center opening and closing hours should be promptly called to account by center management. Further violations must be reported to home offices of chain stores, headquarters of anchor store branches, and directly to the principals of individually owned businesses. The matter is a serious disregard of customer convenience, quite apart from being a violation of a basic condition of the lease agreement that all tenants signed. It erodes customer confidence in the center, while penaliz-

ing those merchants who do adhere to agreed hours and who promote them.

COMMUNITY RELATIONS
"A Community Within a Community" is a trite phrase, yet it is the successful shopping center that can bring this message to its area. Community relations as a phase of shopping center promotion cannot be overemphasized. Any effort that will identify the center closely with the community that surrounds it will have a long-range and highly beneficial effect.

Community relations cannot be casual if they are to succeed. These efforts must be carefully and thoughtfully heeded as an integral part of a promotional program. In these activities the center has the opportunity to project a responsible and neighborly image. The merchants can participate in or sponsor a variety of worthwhile community-oriented events that may provide the use of a community hall, the parking lots, or common areas, before opening or after closing, for social or fund-raising affairs; the center can be used as the site of civic and cultural programs; or merchants can become actively involved in the community activities.

There are any number of ways to make the center part of its community's life and these efforts will pay off in terms of business generated. Community relations activities usually are supervised by the marketing director working under policies established by the developer and a committee of merchants. Committees headed by a local merchant usually help coordinate the center's contribution with those responsible for events.

Community good will is actually an intangible, but it is built upon cumulative actions relating to the community. Here is a checklist of items that go into attaining and maintaining good will:

● If there is a community room, it should regularly be available to local and area civic organizations for meetings, fund raising projects, shows, and other events of a similar nature—at no charge or a very minimal charge. Budget permitting, the merchants association can absorb the preparation and cleanup costs of the events held here.

• Worthwhile fund-raising events for local charities often help a center obtain and secure community identification. It is important, however, that the merchants association, owner-developer, and operations personnel agree in advance on a general policy on the extent of their participation—use of facilities, degree of involvement of center personnel, nature of the event, method of collecting funds, and the like.

Ideally, the center should be opened only to projects and organizations that benefit the entire community. Political rallies, partisan events, and denominational fund raisers frequently are controversial. Often such events encourage requests for "equal time or exposure" from rival organizations.

However, there are no clear guidelines for center management—either from the courts or state and local governments. In the main, opening up the center for public use is an individual decision, and should involve discussion among owner, manager, marketing director, and tenants. The overall policy should be established in advance, preferably before the center even opens.

• For the center desiring to play an active role in the community, there are any number of possibilities. Ideas for community-oriented events are discussed in detail in Chapter 7, but a quick checklist would include: police and fire department exhibits, charity bazaars, band concerts, teachers conventions, regional beauty contests, safety week, charity balls, senior citizens day, career counseling day, mother-daughter day, and father-son day.

As with all shopping center activities, the matter of timing is crucial. Fund-raising and community-oriented events ideally should be scheduled for prepeak or postpeak traffic hours, but never during prime shopping periods. While the building of community good will is extremely important, it should not be accomplished at the expense of decreased traffic or sales in the center stores.

Of the various ways of attaining rapport and good feeling between a shopping center and its community, none is more important than involvement of center and store personnel in community affairs—service clubs, civic groups, religious organizations, charities, and the like. It is an excellent way for the public to more readily accept the center and its staff.

PROMOTING URBAN MALLS
While the construction of new shopping centers and the renovation and expansion of existing ones continue their dominant role in the industry, the development of malls within the central city is gaining momentum. This significant activity is part of a redevelopment process in blighted, decaying areas in most instances, but involves the recycling and renovation of existing buildings and facilities in others.

Addressing the subject of promotion in urban shopping centers, this activity was researched in some recently opened, very successful malls, as well as several others opened within the last decade. An evaluation of their approach and techniques does not reveal startling differences when related to the promotion of conventional suburban shopping centers.

Central city malls have a greater volume of natural customer traffic, resulting from their locations, the advantage of public transportation into the area, as well as large numbers of transients. While these factors result in a definite advantage, it is still necessary to promote the shopping center as an entity, through a merchants association or a promotion fund, controlled by the landlord, and administered by a marketing director.

A comparison of the budgets in an urban vs. a suburban mall would reveal these differences:

• Newspaper costs are greater for an urban mall because full run circulation, rather than zoned editions, are necessary to cover the greater market potential.

• The cost of community relations is smaller in an urban area, because of the greater number of transients, and the fact that the audience is not as sharply segmented as it is in a suburban mall.

• Because of the natural traffic flow previously discussed, the use of devices to lure shoppers into the area is usually minimized in an urban mall.

• Radio and television spots, delivering an institutional message about the inner city mall, are increased to provide continuity to the promotion effort.

The differences in promotion and marketing for an urban vs. a suburban mall are reflected in the emphasis given the various tools used. Although today the media mix chosen generally follows the one outlined, it may change as more urban malls are developed. As the number of these malls increases, experience will be gained in promoting them, and the promotion/marketing techniques will undoubtedly change.

Discussion Questions 5

1. Discuss why a shopping center should be promoted as a unit.

2. How does a marketing director combat factionalism in a merchants association?

3. Outline various alternatives for the marketing director who is faced with some tenants who refuse to participate in promotional activities.

4. Why is advance planning necessary in developing promotion and marketing plans?

5. What steps can be taken to ensure that a promotion is cohesive?

6. What are the pros and cons of uniform store hours for all merchants?

7. Discuss some programs that will help link the center to its community.

8. What are the similarities and differences in promoting urban vs. suburban malls?

6

EFFECTIVE ADVERTISING

One of the most important aspects of the marketing director's job is developing an effective advertising program. A shopping center is a retail development; its survival is dependent on sales. Every element of shopping center promotion is directed at a single goal—getting more people into the center to *buy*. Traffic-generating devices can lure shoppers, but advertising tells them about merchandise that they may wish to own.

Planning advertising for a center is a complex task because of the many elements it embraces. The ads must reach a specific trade area, they must enhance the center's position in the marketplace, and they must be cost-effective. In addition, the advertising budget must be allocated in such a way as to produce a good mix of media—newspapers, special sections, circulars, radio, and television.

Creating the most effective media mix, and getting the most from your advertising budget won't happen automatically. They require ongoing and consistent research and review.

MEDIA BUYING AND SELECTION

Print Media
Print media includes newspapers (daily and weekly), circulars (mail and home deliverance), magazines (regional and local), outdoor billboards, and station posters and transits (buses and taxicabs).

In buying print media, newspapers are the most productive if they meet the desired criteria: daily zoned editions that cover the primary and secondary market areas; a combination of weeklies published on Wednesdays or Thursdays to promote weekend busi-ness; substantial home delivery; insertion of the special section into the newspapers, and a common rate for all shopping center advertisers based on combined, anticipated space usage by shopping center management and tenants.

Zoned advertising, where it is available, is particularly valuable. It enables shopping centers to advertise only in their primary and secondary market areas. This eliminates wasted circulation and usually substantially reduces costs. In addition, by being able to reach a particular market, these ads can be directed to appeal to the specific target audience.

Space contracts—agreements by the center and the media to use a specified amount of space in a given period—are common devices for increasing merchant participation in special newspaper sections and cooperative-page advertising in newspapers. One advantage of these contracts is that smaller merchants who are infrequent advertisers can benefit from lower rates.

The bulk-space contract usually is arranged for and signed by the center's marketing director or agency. The size of the contract can be détermin.ed after securing from tenants estimates of the linage they would use in each of the advertising sections planned during the contract year. By adding the number of institutional ads and cover pages planned by the center to the anticipated gross of merchant advertising, one achieves a reasonably accurate estimate of the size of the contract that should be entered into.

Underusage of the contracted space results in a "short rate" (a charge at a higher rate because of the unused space contracted). If the space contract is exceeded, the next lower rate usually prevails for the amount of space used above the contracted amount. Most marketing directors use a conservative figure in a bulk-space contract in order to avoid "short-rating."

Not all newspapers, however, will offer a rate common to all merchants in the shopping center. While most papers view this as a device that will substantially increase their advertising revenues and convert former nonadvertisers into advertisers, it must be noted that the common rate is usually limited to centerwide events and does not extend to individual merchants for their normal run-of-the-paper advertising. Large advertisers will, of course, use their own contract rate at all times if it is lower than the one offered by the center under a bulk arrangement.

Circulars or Special Newspaper Sections

Most circulars or special newspaper sections are best kept to a tabloid size, even when they are inserts in six- or eight-column newspapers. These circulars create a promotion vehicle for the center that, if properly handled and consistently used, is easily recognizable and read with interest. They can become a potent force in building and maintaining the customer traffic from the prime and secondary market areas.

The cover page of circulars or special sections should be in color, if possible. The cover page is sometimes paid for and sponsored by the merchants association or may be donated by the newspaper publisher. It can be used to publicize an event theme, a general merchandise approach, the days of the promotion, store hours, or the traffic-building device (if any).

The cover states the necessary facts briefly, headlines the merchandise event, and uses attention-grabbing artwork to add impact and to tell the story visually. A simple listing of all tenants is usually ineffective and, hence, a space-waster, although mention of the anchor stores, as space permits, can be helpful. Inclusion of a map or directions to the center is always advisable, but not always possible on the cover. The inside pages of the section are usually devoted to merchandise ads.

Cooperative Pages

Cooperative pages, also called participatory advertising, are good traffic builders if most of the merchants, including the anchor stores, participate. The minimum space goal suggests a double-page spread. This advertising approach, which can be used to create traffic on an otherwise low-volume day, should be limited to a morning or to a one-day event and coordinated with a traffic-building device.

For maximum results, cooperative pages should have an attention-getting banner headline, giving the theme, the day and hours of the promotion, and any other pertinent facts. If pages are divided into equal-sized boxes, and a single typeface is used, an entity is created, rather than a series of individual ads, thus providing the desired mass impact that cannot otherwise be obtained. "Ten Commandments" for this type of effort appear below.

A cooperative page can also be the lead, center, or back page of a circular or a special newspaper section. When incorporated into a section or a circular, the page is usually used for "Early Bird Specials," "Super Values," or similar promotions that add urgency and excitement to the merchandise event.

Overcirculation is frequently cited as a factor in the nonparticipation of merchants in centerwide advertising events, since greater circulation brings additional cost for advertising space at rates that are beyond the means of smaller merchants. Furthermore, saturation that includes the fringes of the trading area rarely results in enough new business to justify the expense.

Overcirculation of promotional advertising is frequently attributable to pressure by the anchor stores, chains, or local merchants who have several units in the area. Although this enables them to promote all stores with a single expenditure, the overall benefit to the center is minimal. While the merchants association can justifiably object to the inclusion of stores in other locations in center circulars, often there is no practical solution to prevent it. The alternative may be that the store will bow out of all center advertising.

In some areas, zoned editions are not available, and marketing directors may not want to spend a large part of the budget on news-

Ten Commandments for Cooperative Pages of Sale Box Ads

1. At least one ad per store—will vary based on the size of the center and the number of cooperative pages. This will help to avoid domination of the pages by anchor stores, provide a more balanced merchant mix, which will, in turn, create more customer traffic.

2. Banner at top of pages—promoting name and location of center, common theme, common sale days, and common store hours.

3. Position of ads to rotate weekly—will give each participating store the opportunity for favorable position of their ads on an equitable basis.

4. Page layout—uniform box ads to be used by every store. Logos not permitted, and store names uniformly at top or bottom of ads in same typeface. This promotes the center as a single entity, rather than as individual merchants.

5. One item only in each ad—this permits clarity and the opportunity to emphasize the merchandise more forcefully.

6. Pricing of sale item—a minimum of 20% less than regular retail price, depending on the timing and importance of the event. Greater minimum reductions for out-of-season and major promotions.

7. Merchandise availability—to be in stock in sufficient quantities with no "bait" advertising.

8. Pre- and Post-Event Pricing—merchandise not to be offered for sale at same price one week before or one week after the advertised event. This will build confidence in the integrity of the promotion.

9. Duplication of items—to be screened by a central committee to avoid competition within the center on a specific item. In the event of duplication, the ad that reached the committee first is published and the other changes to a different item.

10. Participation—by at least 70% of the merchants, including the anchor stores. This will provide the necessary merchant mix and "pull-power" to the pages.

---

paper advertising if circulation extends well beyond the center's trade area. Or, the trade area may be so large or so heavily populated that it is served by several newspapers and thus it would be too costly to advertise in all papers. In these cases, circulars are an alternative to the primary area and to important parts of the secondary market. Distribution is by mail (personal or occupant) or home delivery. The preferred method is by mail, addressed by name, but it is also the most expensive.

Costs will be determined by the number of pages, the quality of paper used, and the circulation method chosen. Unlike newspapers, where space is sold by agate lines or column inches, circulars are offered in increments: 1 page, ½ page (horizontal or vertical), ¼ page, and in some instances, ⅛ page.

There are several problems with direct mail. First, delivery may be erratic; the circular may arrive too early and the customer will have forgotten the circular's contents before the event takes place. If the circular arrives too late, the results are obvious. Another problem is that these mailers are sometimes viewed as "junk" mail and read with half an eye, if at all.

Billboards, transit, and poster advertising are sold by the "showing": the number of units multiplied by the time span, that is 30 units for one month or 15 units for two months or 10 units for 3 months. Billboards should not be overlooked as a good medium for keeping a new center's location in the public's mind.

Radio and Television

Radio offers many choices to the marketing director because of the number of stations available and the diversity of their programming policies. Different stations appeal to different age groups and different cultural and ethnic backgrounds; marketing directors who know the demographic and psychographic characteristics of their trade area keep this in mind when planning advertising programs.

The main advantage of radio is that it reaches potential customers while they are in their cars. If they hear the ad while they are on their way home from work, they may just be induced to drop into the center before they go home. Even if listeners do not make the trip, the radio spot, with a catchy jingle introducing it, keeps a center in the public's mind. So radio can be used to nurture a center's image, bring news of nonmerchandise traffic-building events, and advise, in general terms, of special merchandise offers.

Also of significance when considering the use of radio versus television advertising is that radio ads are much less costly than television ads. Not only is radio time less expensive than television time, but the costs of producing spots is much lower.

This is not to say that television advertising is not worthwhile for shopping centers. It is true that limited budgets, the cost factor, and the inability to zone have, until recently, kept this medium from an even greater share of promotion budgets. However, while cost and zoning continue to be major considerations in the process of media selection, television has, in some areas, begun to claim a greater share of spendable promotion dollars.

This seeming paradox has occurred for several reasons:

• Budgets are increased periodically in most centers and are generally mandated by lease or by merchants association bylaws. The additional funds are used to cover rising costs and for extra exposure in the media beyond what the budget now permits. In many centers, especially those with very large trade areas, the potential impact of television may outweigh or at least balance the cost factor and the inability to zone.

• The large number of stations—network, affiliated, and independent—provide a broad choice of programs and time slots. This offers the potential advertiser an opportunity to schedule spots aimed at specific audiences that will be most motivated to buy the products being promoted.

• More leisure time means more television viewing, with greater exposure for the spots being aired. Astute station selection and scheduling is, of course, vital to the productivity of the spots.

To summarize, there is increasing awareness of the important role television can play in the promotion of shopping centers. However, greater use of this medium must be balanced with good judgment in the selection of stations and the scheduling of promotional spots.

Marketing directors must always keep in mind that there are many factors to evaluate when considering the electronic media: neither radio nor television has the ability to zone into the specific market areas considered prime and secondary by shopping centers. Thus dominance by either medium would depend on program choices offered that would most appeal to potential shoppers, the costs and their effect on the budget, and, of course, acceptance by the merchants and owner-developer.

• Radio and television spots are usually offered in increments of 10, 30, and 60 seconds, and rates for radio are structured to encourage the use of longer announcements. Examples: using 60 second spots as the basis, 10 seconds could cost 50 percent, and 30 seconds 75 percent of the 60 second rate. Television rates do not offer the same cost advantages for the use of longer announcements; 30 seconds will cost 50 percent of 60 seconds, while 10 second rates are usually 50 percent of 30 second costs, a slight price advantage.

Cost-saving devices in buying radio and television time to be considered include:

• Annual contracts guaranteeing minimum air usage. Extend the rates to merchants for their participation in center sponsored events.

• Package deals for a specific number of spots over a specific time period.

• An astute scheduling mix that will correctly reflect the center's market position, but would assure the use of less expensive scheduling, along with some prime time slots. Also, include a specified number of pre-emptibles, which command the lowest rate, but are "bumped" if they can be sold at a higher rate elsewhere.

• Use the smallest number of stations possible, while still covering the primary and secondary market areas. This increases the time on the individual stations, which results in lower rates.

CHOOSING A MEDIA MIX

For any shopping center, the use of media depends on several factors: the location of the center, its trade-radius, and media availability. There is no set formula for producing the *best* media mix for a center; the optimum mix for one center may be disastrous for another. Therefore, the proper mix must be developed by each individual center, after assessing the center's trade area and characteristics of the trade area population.

The local newspapers can supply information about circulation coverage. Audited circulation may be broken down by county or by zip code, which will give the marketing director a good idea of the percent of the trade area covered by the newspaper. Many newspapers also offer selective market coverage. For example, if their actual circulation in the trade area is 70 percent, they will cover the other 30 percent on certain days with inserts from the center, or they will set up a combination of 70 percent delivered and 30 percent mailed. Zoned coverage is, of course, an important option in center advertising programs.

Radio can be effective in reaching specific segments of the market because of the variety of programming the stations offer. If a center is sponsoring an event that will appeal to young people, the key radio station that appeals to them would be a good medium for the message. Radio can be inexpensive for advertising if the marketing director uses it for life style promotion and knows who the target audience is. *Drive times*, 7 to 9 a.m. and 4:30 to 6:30 p.m., are generally the highest rated times. The marketing director who knows the specific appeal of each of the stations in the market can choose the station that will be most effective for an individual promotion.

Television can be a valuable medium if the center has a broad trade area or faces limited competition in the trade area. If television buys are carefully considered so that the center ads achieve a balance between reach and frequency, television can be most effective in selling a concept.

Direct mail can be pinpointed to the center's primary and secondary trade areas and provide maximum coverage. Center special sections can also achieve 100 percent coverage in the trade area if a combination of direct mail and newspaper inserts is used.

Strategically located billboards should not be overlooked as an advertising medium; they can guide customers to the center. Billboards can also be used to advertise special events. The key factor in choosing billboards is location.

With the facts at hand, the marketing director negotiates contracts with the chosen media, making certain that the following important factors are included in the discussions and subsequent agreements.

• The most advantageous rates, based on linage or column inches, (print) frequency, length, time frames (including pre-emptibles) and the availability of package deals (electronic).

• Whether quoted costs are net or gross. Of the latter, the expenditures are commissionable to the merchants association or promotion fund as the "in-house" agency.

• If a "short rate" clause is part of a newspaper contract, it should also include an agreement to charge a lower rate as advertising linage used exceeds the contracted amount.

• Billing at contract rates to be extended to all tenants only during their participation in center-sponsored events.

Successful shopping centers position themselves correctly in their markets through research, then establish and maintain their dominance through an ongoing program of promotion. The mix of factors includes merchandising events, traffic building devices, and community relations, and all are publicized in the media. Thus, thorough research is essential and sound judgment necessary before committing promotion funds. Finally, continuing market research may reveal a change in the demographics, which would, in turn, dictate changes in the use of the media as then constituted.

INSTITUTIONAL VERSUS MERCHANDISE ADVERTISING

Promotion and marketing budgets may provide for two types of advertising; merchandise and institutional advertising. Merchandise advertising is concerned with the sale of goods. Institutional advertising concentrates on image building—keeping the *whole* center in the public's mind.

Merchandise advertising can be broken further into two types: off-price and regular-priced offerings. Off-price merchandise is advertised heavily during natural sale periods such as after Christmas, Washington's and Lincoln's birthdays, after Easter, after July 4, early August, Labor Day, Columbus Day, Election Day, and Veteran's Day. This timing adds a strong promotional pull during normal sale and clearance periods, thus assisting merchants in the disposal of already available reduced merchandise and decreasing the necessity for further costly markdowns. Sale advertising is read with great interest by today's cost-conscious shoppers.

The importance of regular-priced advertising is a source of debate among marketing experts. Some hold that advertising should be limited and advertising dollars saved during periods when customer traffic is normally heavy. Others argue that shoppers must be constantly reminded of a center's variety of merchandise offerings, and regular-priced advertising may draw customers to your center and not the competition. Examples of regular-priced advertising "seasons" are: pre-Easter, pre-summer, Mother's Day and Father's Day, pre-back to school, and pre-Christmas. Clearly, some advertising is important during these periods, but the amount and extent of the promotion is up to the individual center.

Perhaps the greatest source of controversy in advertising is over the value of institutional advertising. Institutional advertising focuses on the center itself, not necessarily on its merchandise. Some retailers, in particular, cannot see the value of spending money in this way, and, admittedly, such advertising does not immediately produce volume increases. Others argue that institutional advertising has a cumulative effect; it stresses the advantages of shopping at a particular center and in so doing, keeps that center in the public eye and it helps it achieve the desired position in the market.

Institutional advertising has one basic message—the image of the center. It may stress accessibility, courtesy, ease of parking, temperature controlled climate, store hours, and variety of shops available—in short, whatever aspects of the center place it in the proper position in customers' minds. If public transportation serves the center, this feature is sometimes cited. In some cases, an institutional ad may simply use eye-catching graphic design to attract the shopper's interest.

Institutional advertising is often combined with merchandise advertising. For example, a page of a special section may be devoted to "selling" the center, while the remainder of the section sells merchandise. In electronic media, the jingle or lead of the ad emphasizes the importance of the center and the remainder of the time is devoted to merchandise or to promoting a special event.

The choice of advertising depends on the individual center and the needs of its market. To be effective, the advertising must be consistent, timely, and attractive. Whether merchandise or institutional advertising is chosen, the goal is the same—to get shoppers into *your* center, not the one next door.

IN-HOUSE VERSUS OUTSIDE AGENCIES

In the early years of shopping centers, the advertising was always handled by outside agencies. The agencies researched and recommended media to the merchant group, sold ad space to tenants, developed a theme for the promotion, handled necessary artwork, provided all pertinent details to the merchants, and arranged to print and distribute special sections. In many locations, the advertising agency also arranged for special nonmerchandise events designed to build center traffic.

Some centers, usually those individually owned, continue to use outside agencies, al-

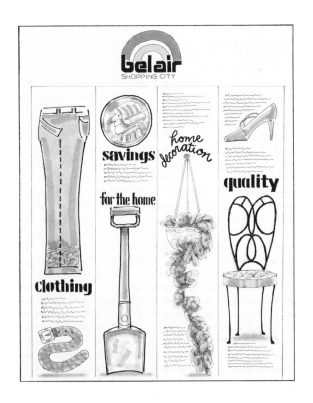

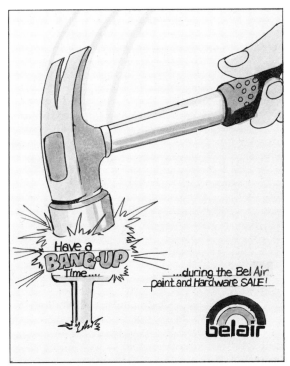

The top left illustration is a rough layout of a cooperative page advertisement. The center's logo is prominently displayed, and the copy describes offerings of individual stores. The full-page ad reflects a consistent, unified design.

The remaining illustrations are sample layouts that could be used as special section covers for off-price merchandise campaigns. Strong graphics like these might also give you ideas for institutional advertisements.

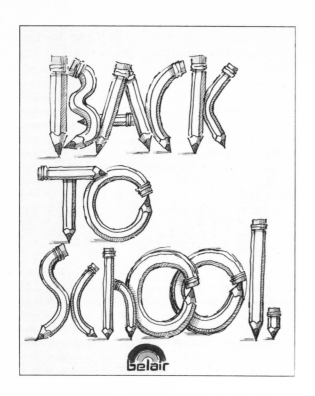

The strongest regular-priced advertising season is, of course, Christmas. You might consider planning an attractive special section, coordinated with advertisements in other media. Three cover ideas are given here.

Back-to-school is another important regular-priced selling season. It is a good time to get full merchant participation in a special advertising section. Other back-to-school cover ideas appear on page 65.

though today marketing directors assume responsibility for most of the items mentioned above. However, many developers with multiple centers have installed in-house agencies that work with the marketing directors on their individual promotion programs. Items covered would include the themes, graphics, copy for cover pages of special sections, coordination of radio and television spots, as well as traffic-building devices.

The plans of the in-house agencies are flexible, based on the needs of specific centers, but they bear a stamp of the shopping center group in the way that they present campaigns and in the quality of production. The standard ad agency fee is returned to the in-house agency and helps support its activities. In many instances, a promotion may be used simultaneously in different centers in more or less identical situations. Where there is a climatic or seasonal difference, it may be used in other centers at different times, but some markets will not adapt to certain promotions in any circumstances.

Where there is doubt about the advisability of using a promotion, the local center should make the decision because of its more intimate knowledge of the market. This is very important because centrally controlled promotion for a group of shopping centers may not present the best individual plan for a specific shopping center. This disadvantage should not, of course, be allowed to offset the many advantages offered by in-house promotion: tighter control, quality presentation, innovative ideas, and lower costs. It should be stressed, however, that in-house agencies are practical in the operation of shopping center groups, not individual centers, because the cost of individual attention would negate the other advantages.

Discussion Questions 6

1. Outline the criteria for the selection and mix of media for center advertising. Discuss them.

2. Describe the different types of print media available and the advantages of each.

3. Describe the advantages and disadvantages of radio and television advertising.

4. What are the elements of a good special section cover?

5. What are the most important elements in insuring that cooperative box ads are productive?

6. With advertising rates rising steadily, discuss ways to cut costs—for newspapers, radio, and television.

7. What is the role of institutional advertising for shopping centers?

8. What are the advantages and disadvantages of in-house advertising agencies?

7

PLANNING CENTERWIDE PROMOTION ACTIVITIES

Consistent, aggressive, on-going programs of publicity and promotional activity—properly timed and well coordinated—are the key ways to generate a sustained flow of customers to a center and its stores. With that truism out of the way, how does the promotion/marketing director achieve this desired result?

Plans and budgets are the first steps, and they necessarily go hand in hand. The gross available funds can easily be determined by looking at the total merchant dues and the developer contribution. Next, a comprehensive program fully geared to the promotional needs of the center must be formulated and must include the greatest number of merchandise promotions and traffic-building events that the budget can allow. It is here that the marketing director has maximum opportunity to create, improvise, weigh, and digest all of the promotional techniques he or she can devise or learn from peers. Special events should have local appeal where possible, and marketing directors must always add a measure of their own creativity to other promotions.

The association's bylaws usually require presentation and approval of the program (before the full association, a promotion committee, or the board of directors). It is at this key stage that the promotion director must demonstrate an ability to communicate well, a knowledge of the center, its stores, and its customers—both existing and potential. Under the promotion fund concept, a merchant steering committee should be consulted, but this is not mandatory.

In formulating the program, great care and

judgment must be exercised to make each event productive. It is better to spend time, effort, and money on a few well-timed major events than to schedule numerous promotions, some of which are poorly timed and poorly prepared, and consequently nonproductive. The realistic approach is to develop a full schedule of events, based on need, then eliminate the least important ones as necessary to meet the budget.

If this is the center's first full year of operation, the success of the preopening, Grand Opening, and 30-day postopening promotion programs must be reviewed. After these events tenants are particularly sensitive; those that did well in the first month or so are eager to continue this trend; others may await with anxious concern what real business may in fact await them once the center returns to "normal routine."

Poor communication between tenants and the merchants association (or promotion unit) always adversely affects merchant participation in centerwide promotions. Therefore, it is essential to notify merchants well in advance and include complete details relating to each event. Incomplete details and the late receipt of the information are excellent excuses for unenthusiastic tenants who want to avoid participation.

It is important, at this point, to clearly distinguish between two basic types of promotional event: merchandising events and special events. Merchandising events—the darling of retailers—are built around traditional buying periods and stress goods and merchandise, seasonal or clearance. Simply put, they are designed to get customers in the mood to buy.

Special events are those promotions geared to attract crowds, who will, it is hoped, become buyers. Less mercantile in nature, they nevertheless play a vital role in continuing to remind the trading area of the center's existence. Admittedly, the distinctions are purist; one hopes that all promotional efforts produce higher sales for all merchants, and merchandising events and special events both have important roles to play in the center's total program. These two types can be molded together to present individual promotion programs that combine the best of both approaches.

The timing of merchandise promotions often determines their productivity. After fully recognizing the importance of department store participation and the need to coordinate the scheduling of center merchandise events with anchors' efforts, certain factors must also be a part of the discussion and thinking that take place before the schedule of cooperative centerwide merchandise events is completed.

1. Adequate budgets must be allocated for publicizing the events. This would include cover pages for special sections or mailers, radio or television spots starting during the evening preceding the first day, and teaser ads.

2. The timing of merchandise events must be coordinated. A well-balanced schedule will ensure the greatest possible interest, and the major stores will usually participate in promotions that complement or coincide with their own event calendars. Their cooperation naturally triggers strong merchant support.

Here are some classic "do's" and "don'ts" for timing these events.

Do schedule sale merchandise events to coordinate with those planned by department stores.

Do schedule merchandise events for natural clearance periods: after Christmas, Lincoln's birthday, Washington's birthday, after Easter, after July 4th, after Back-to-School, and so on.

Do schedule sale merchandise events for other historically important shopping periods: Anniversary Sale, Columbus Day, Veteran's Day, and so on.

Don't schedule sale-merchandise events for natural peak selling periods: Thanksgiving through Christmas, three weeks prior to Easter or Back-to-School, and two weeks preceding Mother's Day and Father's Day, etc. Advertising of regular priced merchandise should be planned at this time.

Don't schedule peak-selling-period merchandise promotions instead of off-peak-period events if the budget cannot support both, or if merchant participation in the peak-period event will affect the off-peak effort.

Because there are different schools of thought on timing and merchandising, the "do's" and "don'ts" are controversial and an explanation is in order. In the simplest possible terms, most merchants cannot afford to participate in every merchandising effort. If given a choice, they are more likely to participate when customer traffic is not normally at its peak; at this time stores can benefit from the stimulation of a promotion.

Critics inevitably point to competition from nearby centers and the need for constant merchandise promotion to increase customer flow, particularly during high-volume periods. To the degree that the merchants association or promotion fund budget will permit, institutional advertising via radio or television spots, and traffic-building devices properly publicized, can be used during non-merchandise promotion periods. These efforts should also be supplemented with other innovative "happenings" that will bring additional traffic to the mall.

There are numerous traffic-building devices —free or costly, good or bad. But they do represent a building block on which to base supplementary promotional efforts when, for whatever reason, merchandise events are not the best choice, or require an assist.

Ideally, most merchandising events— Anniversary Sales, Sidewalk Sales, After-Christmas and After-Easter Clearances, Washington's Birthday Sales, Summer Clearances, Columbus Day, Veteran's Day, Election Day—should be accompanied by exhibits or shows. However, powerful merchandise events require little or no supplement, and in these instances a major portion of the budget should be allocated to "ballyhooing" the merchandise effort. This means cover pages for special sections, radio or television spots, teaser ads, and so forth. Conversely, merchandise events with less inherent "pull" require greater expenditures for traffic-building.

During natural high-volume periods—pre-Christmas, pre-Easter, pre-Mother's Day, pre-Father's Day, pre-Back-to-School—the emphasis must be on traffic-building devices in an effort to capture more than the normal share of customer traffic. The devices chosen must draw customer traffic in greater-than-usual volume and should be timed to lure customers into the center earlier in the day than is normal, or near the closing hour, which will delay their departure. This technique leaves shoppers free to shop instead of being entertained during the peak hours, permits stores to schedule their personnel appropriately, and, most importantly, provides a reason for more shoppers to reach the center earlier or remain later, thus building more shopping hours into the day.

Timing is vital when planning special events. Always remember to give visitors enough time to become customers. On-the-mall special events tend to keep potential customers on the mall and out of the stores. Indoor shows held in the community hall or auditorium create a captive audience and half-hour events invariably develop into longer shows. If the scheduling conflicts with prime shopping time during the late afternoon or early evening, viewers may depart the center for home because little time for shopping remains.

An intelligent professional approach to merchandising promotions will help increase the amount of customer traffic and can result in subsequent substantial increases in volume. But traffic-building devices used as supplements to major merchandise promotions, or as main events, also contribute to the center's success. The varied examples that follow are tried and proven, the situation, the need, the time, and, last but not least, the budget dictate which is the most favorable event.

Basically, the traffic-building devices fall into three categories:

• As supplements to *major* merchandise promotions, at little or no cost to the merchants association.

• As additional vehicles to support merchandising promotions that are not very important, at moderate cost to the merchants association.

• As catalysts to motivate shoppers to visit your center instead of a competitive shopping center within the primary and secondary market areas. Larger expenditures are necessary and justified in these circumstances.

LOW-BUDGET OR NO-BUDGET EVENTS

Supplements to Major Merchandise Promotions

Flower Shows. Invite the community garden clubs to exhibit their flowers on the mall. Displays should be in all areas of the shopping center and not concentrated in one or two locations. As an added incentive, the flowers could be offered for sale to the viewing public, with the proceeds donated to a local charity chosen by the sponsoring organization.

Automobile and Boat Shows. Time these shows to coincide with the unveiling of new models; give credits in the attendant publicity to the participating dealers; and be sure that exhibits are set up throughout the shopping center to assure a flow of traffic to all areas.

Arts and Crafts Exposition. A demonstration by area students of their skills in painting, drawing, pottery, silkscreening, weaving, and other crafts. Local and area schools are invited to ask their students to participate in this event, which is held as a supplement to a centerwide sale, but will, on its own, produce a substantial amount of additional shopper traffic.

Students practice their crafts at tables set up throughout all sections of the common areas, with each category identified by a table sign. Each school receives a suitably engraved trophy in recognition of their participation in this project. The production cost is minimal, consisting of rental charges for the tables, purchase of the trophies, and lunch for the exhibitors.

Here is a low-budget, community-oriented event that should be publicized in center advertising and/or radio-television spots. Its value in building good will for any center that seeks close identification with local activities cannot be overstated.

Ticket Wednesday (or any day). Choose the slowest day of the week to run cooperative merchandise advertising. Follow the guidelines included with Chapter 6, "Ten Commandments for Cooperative Pages of Sale Box Ads," and get as much merchant participation as possible.

The pages should be headed "Ticket Wednesday," the sale event for Wednesday only, and a coupon with space for name, address, and telephone number must appear in the center of each cooperative page. Shoppers clip, complete, and deposit their coupons in a box located in a central mall area on Wednesdays.

Twenty-five winners are selected from the box by random drawing on the following day, and they each receive a pair of tickets to an event: movies, theater, hockey, baseball, basketball, football games, wrestling, and so forth. Tickets are purchased by the merchants association or promotion fund and presented to the winners in advance of the event date.

This low-cost event can be used to build traffic and volume on an otherwise slow day. It can run weekly, every other week, or monthly.

Crime Prevention Week: Set up displays and lectures on the subject with local law enforcement agencies at the local, county, and state levels. The material should cover all phases of police work, with special emphasis on crime prevention. Arrange for demonstrations of the specific skills of police-sponsored organizations.

Material displayed can be concentrated into a central mall area if it is not too massive, or shown throughout the entire mall if it is extensive. Demonstrations and lectures should be held in normally low traffic periods, and scheduled for times that will bring shoppers to the mall earlier than usual, and keep them later.

This low-cost event is community-oriented,

and can be used to supplement traffic generating sale periods. Be sure to publicize it in advance by including the details in centerwide advertising and/or radio-television spots that run in conjunction with a sale event. Use small ads and/or radio-television spots to promote it, if there is no other centerwide advertising scheduled for crime prevention week.

Police and Fire Department Exhibits. Display the newest equipment and feature lectures on the latest techniques in use, with question-and-answer sessions scheduled for certain times. Representatives of the police or fire department should be on hand at the exhibit at all times.

Band Concerts. Every community has one or more musical groups—sponsored by local schools, clubs, civic organizations, or police and fire departments—and every shopping center is surrounded by communities that constitute its prime and secondary market areas. Invite their bands or orchestras to perform—the center's invitation indicates community awareness and its acceptance is a recognition that the center is indeed a part of the community.

Good timing will help to accomplish the hoped-for increase in customer traffic. But avoid the poor scheduling that can create a "captive" audience during the prime shopping hours—the audience will be listening and not shopping.

Conventions. Highly beneficial to the customer-traffic pattern, conventions can boost volume in centers close to the convention site. Newspaper advertising or radio spots should welcome guests and invite them to visit the center by interesting them in special activities and by promoting the good will of the community.

Publicize added incentives that will help both traffic and volume. For example, if there is a teachers' convention, set up an apple cart centrally on the mall, with a large sign proclaiming. "An apple for the teacher—Compliments of Bel Air Mall." In addition, one or more cooperative pages of box ads with "Welcome Teachers" banners can transform visitors into buyers. The center will benefit further if regular mall shoppers are attracted by the promotion.

Regional Beauty Contests. Beauty contests are excellent traffic builders that also contribute to community good will. The center can be the site of an area or county contest, either related or unrelated to state or nationwide beauty pageants. All activities should be held in the auditorium if one is available, or in a central mall area if not.

The publicity campaign heralding the contest should use radio or TV spots, the cover page of a mailer, or a newspaper insert to both promote merchandise and give news coverage of the contest, which will be of interest to the entire community.

As the supplement to a significant merchandising promotion, the beauty contest must be well timed. Because of the interest it will stimulate in the local community, it inevitably will produce a substantial amount of additional traffic. This technique can keep the mall fully trafficked for more hours than normal.

It is preferable to schedule the contest for the off-peak periods, since an event of this type creates a completely captive audience.

Charity Bazaars. These are among the most productive low-cost traffic-building devices ever used by shopping centers. In this instance, "productive" is a multifaceted term, because a charity bazaar attracts a vast number of additional mall shoppers while serving simultaneously as a builder of community good will.

Follow these guidelines when planning a charity bazaar:

• Select a date that will be acceptable to the major charitable organizations in the area. Enclosed all-weather malls can schedule the bazaar at a mutually acceptable time, regardless of weather. Open shopping centers must consider the weather if booths, tables, and racks are to be set up in the open mall areas.

• Of course, the bazaar must be properly timed to complement the centerwide merchandise promotion that will accompany it.

Peak sales periods should be avoided. Also avoid planning bazaars for times when shopping is normally light. Weeks with holidays—for example, Election Day, Veteran's Day, Lincoln's and Washington's Birthdays, and Memorial Day—are excellent choices because schools are closed on the holidays and customer traffic normally increases.

• Community organizations should invite all the major charities within the prime and secondary trading areas to participate. Avoid "fringe" groups because it is not possible for everyone to be included. Overcrowding will strain the available facilities; it will also weaken the presentation and cause traffic congestion on the mall walkways that could add up to more "shoppers" than buyers.

• Needless to say, it is important to verify the authenticity of those charitable organizations that apply for participation, if not invited, and the Better Business Bureau or Chamber of Commerce are the most reliable agencies for this purpose. The major criteria are that the group be a member of the community, nonprofit, and expend funds raised from this and similar projects for the exclusive benefit of the community. These same regulations, of course, apply to those organizations specifically invited.

• Ground rules should be mapped out in advance and clear to all who take part. Participating charities may use the designated areas of the mall to sell their products and wares. Food items, plants, flowers, pottery, knit goods, embroidered or crocheted articles are some of the items that may be sold. Merchandise and food (if health regulations permit) are displayed on tables, booths, and racks usually supplied by the shopping center at no cost to the user. Participating organizations are restricted to designated areas and may use signs identifying their groups. For uniformity in size and look, the shopping center should arrange for preparation of the material. If the merchants association fund can absorb the cost, this will further promote good will. If it is not possible, participating organizations pay for their own materials, but should cooperate to achieve the uniformity described above.

Health Fairs. These events are most often held

in one or more central mall areas. There are usually extensive displays and free tests for blood pressure, glaucoma, and other common illnesses. A blood bank van to accept blood donations, the collection of used eyeglasses, movies on alcoholism, demonstrations of artificial respiration, and similar activities are common to such fairs. A fair may be one to three days long and can run concurrently with the merchandise event. Local or state agencies are usually cooperative and eager to participate.

Building University Good Will. Every shopping center with universities and colleges in the primary or secondary trading areas should woo the students, faculty, and other employees. Their good will, in accepting the center as an integral part of the community, can mean a large "plus" in customer traffic that translates into added dollar volume.

The support of the university can be gained by a well-thought-out, forcefully executed program that would include

• Consistent advertising in the college newspaper.

• Pep rallies for the athletic teams to be held in the shopping center, with players, coaches, cheerleaders, fraternity and sorority members present. They should be held during normally low-customer-traffic periods, utilizing a parking lot or a centrally located area of the mall. Adequate publicity will increase the turnout, since this can be an exciting event for many local residents as well.

• Offering part-time employment to college students and using the college newspaper for advertisements when positions are open.

Safety Week. This week-long event includes displays that compare safe and unsafe bicycles, motorcycles, and automobiles; helmets and goggles as reminders to motorcycle riders; demonstrations in the proper use of safety belts; explanations of traffic laws; and common-sense safety rules that are essential to the event.

Local officers should be stationed at the center during the week-long clinic to answer questions and to assist citizens in their safety checks. Advice on safeguarding property could also be a part of the program.

Charity Balls. These are outstanding events that can be one of the vehicles used to make any shopping center a part of the community. The ground rules are simple, the cost minimal, and the benefits enormous. Beneficiaries of the event would be local, nonprofit organizations that function for the good of the community; for example, the local hospital, the volunteer fire department, or the Red Cross. The ball is usually scheduled to start after the mall closes on a Saturday night, with the main concourse transformed into a ballroom by the sponsoring organization, assisted by shopping center personnel.

In addition to donating the use of the "ballroom" and parking lots, the merchants association sometimes makes a contribution to the expenses (orchestra, refreshments, if permitted by law, etc.), which increases the profit derived from the event. However, such a donation is wholly dependent on the budget, because free use of the facilities will, in itself, enhance the relationship of the center and the community.

A charity ball, while not traffic-building for a specific merchandise promotion, can have a strong cumulative effect for the future. It can, in fact, be used at the conclusion of a weekend event and be publicized in the appropriate advertisements.

Men's Night. This inexpensive volume-building device can be used during the gift-giving pre-Christmas and pre-Mother's Day periods. Timed for an evening approximately two weeks before the holidays, use teaser and merchandise ads to proclaim the upcoming event. Some centers run Men's Night during the normal evening shopping hours, while others extend their closings for one or two hours to accommodate the promotion.

Incentives that should be publicized can include a specially priced item from each participating store, free coffee and dessert, or token gifts for each male shopper. Specially designated hostesses should be available for guidance on the mall and in the stores, to make the shopping easy and pleasant.

The traffic-builders outlined can be implemented at minimal cost and are productive when used to supplement *major* merchandise events. Used as auxiliaries, they strongly support the merchandise effort but are less than effective when promoted as the main events.

MODERATE-COST PROMOTIONAL EVENTS

Senior Citizen's Day. This is a noteworthy event that is designed to build good will. Such a program aids a center in gaining acceptance as an integral part of the community. While volume increases should be evident on Senior Citizen's Day as a result of increased mall traffic, the greatest benefit to be derived is from the cumulative effect of these special days if they are scheduled with consistency and promoted with imagination. The program should include the following:

• Adequate publicity using newspaper and radio spots, which will provide the details.

• If a merchandise promotion is scheduled for that same day, the facts should appear in the advertising and radio spots.

• Free (or subsidized) transportation to the shopping center should be provided together with a free (or subsidized) movie if the center includes a theater.

• Lunch at reduced prices, as well as discounts, not exceeding 20%, on specific merchandise items to be offered during the hours Senior Citizens are on the mall.

The presentation of a Medicare card is essential for participation. Remember successful shopping centers build and maintain community goodwill. Senior Citizen's Days can be part of the "mix" for early acceptance as a welcome neighbor.

"Play Money" Auction. This relatively inexpensive traffic-building device can be used most successfully to supplement a less-than-major merchandise promotion. Cost may be borne by the merchants association or shared with tenants, depending on the availability of association funds.

Here is how the auction works.

• Plan the auction in conjunction with a three-day (or more) merchandise promotion ending on a Saturday night.

• The merchants association should print "play money" in various denominations, to be ready in advance of the start of the merchandise promotion.

• During the sale event, customers receive play money from the participating stores in the exact amounts of their purchases.

• Depending on its size and volume, each store contributes merchandise to be sold at auction at the time and place specified on Saturday night. These items should be publicized and described on the cover page of the newspaper section promoting the merchandise event, also in teaser ads or radio spots. All available items are sold to the highest bidders, who must pay for their purchases in play money only. This fact should be made clear in all announcements.

Strong merchant participation, advance publicity, and an adequate number of articles for auction are the necessary ingredients for a successful promotion. (Be sure to check lottery laws.)

Weekend in New York (or Other City) Prizes. This device is an interesting companion to a nonmajor merchandise promotion. A weekend for two in a large city located in a different geographic area always adds excitement to any merchandise promotion and stimulates an additional flow of traffic to the center.

The rules and procedures are uncomplicated.

Prizes

A weekend in New York (or other city) that includes hotel, dinners, and theater tickets for six winning couples.

Drawing

To be held on Saturday at 6 p.m. or on the last day of the merchandise promotion. Winners are notified by mail or telephone.

Coupons

Customers will receive one coupon for each purchase of $5 or more at any center store. Name, address, and telephone number are filled in by the customer. The coupons must be deposited in official collection boxes on the mall or in the stores. On-the-mall depositories are preferable because they keep traffic flowing between stores. (Be sure to check any local lottery laws that may regulate this.)

On-Mall Promotion

Window and interior signs should be placed in all stores, briefly giving contest details.

Advertising
• Teaser ads several days prior to the merchandise event and the start of coupon distribution.

• A special merchandise section. Use the cover page to promote the merchandise event and the "Trip to New York" giveaway.

• An announcement ad about the drawing on the day before it takes place.

Career-Counseling Day. This event is completely oriented to the community and can be one in a series of good-will builders.

Depending on the geographical size of the primary and secondary market areas, the program that follows can be sponsored by any shopping center:

• Counseling services for job training and job opportunities conducted by representatives of the state employment agency, privately owned agencies, and others with expertise in the field.

• Interviews with personnel directors of leading area industries or businesses offering guidance on specific available job opportunities, both current and upcoming. Qualifications for those positions and information on any available training facilities would be discussed with the interviewers.

• Area college admission offices would be invited to participate in the programs by arranging appointments in advance, through local high schools, for seniors with college plans. Depending on the budget, out-of-area admissions officers may also be invited. However, such college counseling is generally conducted at individual area high schools, and these efforts may be a needless repetition. Hold these meetings in one central area to expedite the interviews and avoid repetition.

The community room can be used as the setting for the career counseling on employment, training, and college; this space should be offered free of charge.

News of the meetings should be announced in newspaper advertising, in radio spots, and by word of mouth at the area high schools and employment agencies. Adequate publicity ensures good attendance and, in turn, adds to the stature of the center among local residents.

To build further interest in this civic activity, those attending the counseling sessions should be given the opportunity to win a wardrobe appropriate for campus or career. The contest procedures are simple:

• Complete details of the drawing should be given in the preliminary publicity. Coupons are then printed, with spaces for the name, address, and telephone number of the recipient. A coupon is given to each attendant at the conclusion of his or her session. The collection boxes are placed in the meeting room, and a random drawing is held at the conclusion of the series of counseling sessions. (Check local and state lottery laws before planning the event.)

• Winners would receive gift certificates in varying amounts that would be valid only for articles of clothing (the gift certificate should so state) chosen from the center store of their choice. The gift certificates used would be immediately redeemable for cash from the merchants association, which would absorb the cost of the clothing.

• While this event is a good supplement to a merchandise promotion, it will not generate a great amount of additional customer traffic on its own. However, it can be a valuable tool for building and maintaining community good will.

Arrival of Santa. This annual event is usually timed for the Friday after Thanksgiving, the traditional start of Christmas shopping. The arrival, in recent years, has often been by helicopter, and, while this is not unusual, the "happening" can be developed into an exciting affair with the addition of one or more supplementary promotional devices.

You could arrange for the helicopter to drop 300 to 500 ping pong balls, painted in different colors and numbered, over the shopping center site. Finders take the balls from store to store until they match colors and numbers. A predetermined prize, donated by the merchant, is given to those who locate stores with matching colors and numbers.

This is only one example of the many and varied supporting promotions that can be utilized. Marketing directors should use their creativity in designing this promotion, giving it as much local appeal as possible. Under any circumstances, they must make certain to publicize Santa's arrival to the fullest, by inserting the message into radio and television spots, and utilizing the cover page of the Christmas special section usually timed for Thanksgiving Day. In the unlikely event a promotion is not planned, create it with special messages.

Dog-gone Good Competition. Dog lovers represent a large segment of any community, and a contest among dogs is certain to "wow" them. Here's how it works: run small newspaper ads inviting owners to enter their dogs in either or both of two contests.

Pet dogs are dressed in costumes, and prizes are awarded for the best dressed, as well as the first and second runners-up. Separately, a prize is given for the sexiest, prettiest, ugliest, and the cutest. Judges can be chosen from among those who show dogs, or any animal lover can serve. Prizes are for the dogs, not the owners, and can include any item of apparel or equipment.

Schedule the contest for low customer traffic periods, over two or three days, depending on the number of entrants involved. Use it as a supplement to a centerwide merchandise promotion, describing the contest on the cover page of the special section, or as a separate traffic builder.

This moderate-cost promotional event will not only add customer traffic, but can also build good will because it relates to the community. Marketing directors can garnish this idea with their own creativity for an exciting crowd pleaser.

Vacation Week. This promotional program should coincide with summer vacation planning, which would place this event in May or early June.

The vacation theme should be part of a complete package including the merchandising effort, the displays, the prizes, and so forth. Here are some guidelines to use in developing such a program.

• Schedule a merchandise event for the last three days of vacation week. Promote it with a special section that has a cover page exploiting the theme.

• Use on-the-mall exhibits that will repeat the word "vacation," for example: "vacation boats," "vacation camping equipment," and so on. Decorate the displays with interesting travel posters or anything that can inspire shoppers to think about their vacation plans and needs.

• Invite travel agents to participate in "vacation week" and set up booths on the mall for dispensing information, answering questions, and booking trips. (Check local and state lottery laws.)

• Offer trips as prizes, with the drawing to be made on the last day of the exhibit. The drawing should be well publicized, scheduled for a nonpeak period, and presided over by a local celebrity.

• The costs of the trips are sometimes paid by travel agents, in whole or in part. If it is not possible to make this arrangement with agents, it can be paid for out of the promotion fund.

Properly coordinated and aggressively promoted, this combination of merchandise promotion and traffic-building device can be very successful.

Mother-Daughter Day. Time this event for a two- or three-day weekend preceding Mother's Day, but not for the weekend of Mother's Day. A week or two before the date is probably best.

Prepare a budget for this event. Here is a suggested outline for the program.

● Invite hairstylists, cosmeticians, and fashion coordinators from among the center's tenants, or contact specialists from the prime or secondary market areas who are available for consultation.

● These consultants can be reimbursed from the promotion budget; the payment should not exceed normal charges.

● Consultations could be held in an area that is easily sectioned off, to provide the necessary privacy. Individual areas of consultation can be created by using booths or screens, as well as chairs, tables, and mirrors, which may be rented if they are not normally available.

● This event can be well publicized by using radio spots, teaser ads, the cover page of a special Mother's Day merchandise section, or the banner of cooperative pages (see below).

● Give favors to the first 1,000 mothers accompanied by their daughters. A carnation would be an appropriate gift that could also fit the budget.

An accompanying merchandise promotion, timed with the beauty consultations described above, would be a good plan—and a productive one. Announce the promotion in a newspaper insert or in a tabloid with a cover page describing the Mother-Daughter Days. As an alternate use cooperative pages with a banner briefly outlining the on-going mall events.

Father-Son Days. This event is similar to Mother-Daughter Days, but limited to one or two days. If the promotion is scheduled for a Saturday (or Sunday) it will produce a good deal of traffic because these are not, for most people, work days.

● Feature personal appearances by sports figures or athletic teams in the area. The guests could talk informally about their teams, other players, their own experiences, their ambitions, and so on. Appearances can be followed by short question-and-answer periods and an autograph-signing session.

● Arrange demonstrations by the sports figures, perhaps to instruct the audience on the proper use of athletic equipment. Again, choose athletes affiliated with teams that are supported by area residents.

● Hold a drawing for several prizes of athletic equipment donated by center merchants or purchased by the merchants association. Another prize should be season tickets for two to all home games of the favorite athletic team in the area. (Check state and local lottery laws.)

● Schedule the random drawing just prior to the peak traffic hours, but sufficiently early to avoid interference with shopping during the prime buying period. The event would be publicized by an ad providing all the details and including a coupon to be deposited in boxes located in each store. All ballots would later be gathered into one large box located in a central location on the mall. The drawing should be made by a well-known area sports personality.

Although Father-Son Day will not, in itself, contribute substantially to volume, if the timing is right and the costs are moderate, it is an event that can further good will by identifying the center as an integral part of the community and a source of entertainment without burdening the budget. An accompanying merchandise promotion stressing Father's Day gifts would be beneficial to the merchants and helpful to the shoppers. This could be in the form of a double-page spread following the Father-Son Day announcement page, with a strong banner identifying the promotion plus equal-sized boxes for merchandise advertisements.

Mystery Photographs. This is another moderate- to low-cost traffic-generating event. Use it in conjunction with an advertised merchandise promotion.

● An unidentified photographer takes pictures of individual shoppers during the sale event.

Photos are snapped during the first two days of a three-day promotion.

• Pictures are then displayed in a central area of the mall, and this fact is publicized in advance on the cover page of the event's special section. In addition, announcements are made over the centerwide public address system, giving the location of the photographic display.

• Shoppers who identify their photographs within the specified time period receive gift certificates or prizes. These are donated by participating merchants or purchased with the association's promotional funds.

Using the mystery photographer is not costly nor is it a complex program. It can, however, create excitement during a merchandise promotion.

All of these events are well-tested, productive programs that can augment merchandise promotions that require some supportive action. The production costs are moderate and can be controlled by limiting or expanding the scope of each individual event. There are many more promotions that could be included with this group, and new ideas are being developed almost daily. The events described here are only a sampling and can be adapted for use by specific centers to meet their own requirements. In the creation of further traffic-builders, or in their adaptation, every effort should be made to inject or retain as much local flavor as possible—know your shoppers and what they like, whether it's music or baseball teams.

HIGH-COST SPECIAL EVENTS THAT CREATE CUSTOMER TRAFFIC

High-cost special events are used only during peak periods. They may be scheduled for a time when there is no other specific merchandise promotion, or they can be the predominant event during a minor merchandise promotion. The costs of these events must be controlled by each shopping center's budget. The programs must be aimed at the largest possible audience, timed to the season, and reflect as much local color as possible. Some productive traffic-building devices are listed below.

Antique Show. This can be an exciting presentation of great interest to many shoppers. Displays are available through those agents that specialize in shopping center promotion and since they are in great demand they should be scheduled well in advance. Some agents will charge the center a fee to bring in a show; others may actually pay the center for the use of the mall. Either way, be certain that the show's sponsor is professionally capable.

Soap Opera Excitement. The current hysteria over daytime soap operas has spilled over into the shopping center industry. Daytime soaps boast a viewing audience of approximately 7,000,000, and 70 percent of the viewers are women. Because women are the motivating force in the shopping habits of their families, a traffic-building device related to soap operas is a "natural," and a powerful instrument with which to build center traffic to an absolute peak.

The special event involves guest appearances by soap opera personalities, and these appearances have generated large, enthusiastic and sometimes hysterical crowds. Recently, a leading newspaper reported that a screaming, weeping crowd of 2,000 greeted the female and male stars of a currently popular soap opera. They had to be restrained by security guards, and it was necessary to escort the performers to their cars afterwards because of the enthusiasm of the crowd.

This is an act now booked in shopping centers across the country, which invariably produces the desired results—a large outpouring of spectators, who can be converted into customers if the event is properly handled and well publicized.

The factor most important to its success and productivity is the one that appears very frequently throughout the book—*timing*. Schedule the appearances during off-peak traffic hours, 11 a.m. to 12 noon, and 6 p.m. to 7 p.m. weekdays. The traffic pattern on Saturdays is different, and the performance should be timed from 11 a.m. to 12 noon, and 9 p.m. until closing. Because this act will create a "captive" audience, the times mentioned will entice viewers to the mall earlier than usual, keep them later, and offer the opportunity to shop between appearances of the personalities.

Preparations are minimal, requiring a stage set up in a central area of the mall, microphones, and spotlights. Because of the excitement it may be necessary to augment the center's security force and use restraining ropes or chains.

This is a relatively high cost event, to be used as a primary traffic builder in persuading consumers to visit your mall instead of the neighboring one. To reach the objective of a mass buildup of visitors, it must be publicized to the degree permitted by the budget. Use "teaser" ads, 10- or 20-second television and 30-second radio spots at least 2 days prior to the appearances of the stars. On the preceding day, announce the details, making certain the performance times are prominently mentioned.

This is not an event that depends on merchandising to build customer traffic, and a special section is unnecessary. The use of cooperative pages, with each merchant offering a special for the day of the show only, could persuade more viewers to shop while in the center, even though they have not intended to. However, most of them will, with or without merchandise advertising, if given the opportunity to do so by judicious timing of the special event.

Courtesy Campaign for Store Employees. As a sustained, traffic-producing device, a courtesy campaign can achieve important long-term results.

The reasons for emphasizing courtesy are self-evident. Shoppers will return to a center regularly if the atmosphere is friendly and the service courteous. However, even a minority of employees in a minority of the stores can create a poor image for the center, whereas it takes the overwhelming majority of employees in a majority of stores to establish and maintain the image of courtesy, friendliness, service, and those other intangibles that lead customers to make the center a shopping habit.

You may wish to underscore the importance of courtesy by giving employees some proven sales attitudes that will sell customers . . . directly to the *competition*:

• **Be rude.** If shoppers are uncertain about what they want, why waste your time . . . do they think you are there to help them?

• **Don't offer service to your customers.** Maybe they'll go away and you won't be bothered with making out a sales slip and completing a sale.

• **Don't accept returns.** If customers decide they don't like their purchases or if they don't fit, that's not your fault! Why, then, is the customer bothering you?

• **Don't shop your competition.** If their stores are heavily trafficked and yours is empty, it could be the way your salespeople comb their hair. Your competitors can't have better management or personnel; they're just lucky, and it's probably just temporary.

• **Close early.** Be sure your customers know you have more important things to do than to be of service to them.

Reproduced below is the entire kit of instructions and forms necessary to undertake a campaign to enhance the friendliness and courtesy of store employees (but check state and local laws before using). The instructions are self-explanatory. It will be relatively easy to get people interested in this campaign because both customers and employees have a chance to win.

Courtesy Campaign Instruction Kit

This kit contains everything you should have—or know about—for our mallwide courtesy campaign.

1. Rules and regulations governing the awarding of prizes for courteous service rendered by store employees.

2. A list of prizes for customers and store employees.

3. The copy that will appear in newspaper advertising, promoting our month-long courtesy campaign.

4. Courtesy campaign *identification badges*.

READ THE ENCLOSED MATERIAL
CAREFULLY

More important, help us make this courtesy campaign a rousing success so it will benefit everyone's volume now, and later too. The more you smile, the more courteous and helpful you are to your shoppers, the more votes you get, and the better your chances are to win a valuable prize. If you lose your badge or any of the enclosed material, please obtain a replacement from the Marketing Director.

Note: The following rules will appear on all official courtesy campaign ballots. Additional instructions for store employees follow these rules.

RULES AND REGULATIONS

1. All votes must be cast on official ballots and must be completely filled out in order to be eligible.

2. All ballots must be deposited at official polling booths prior to 5:00 p.m., Saturday,   (date) , under the supervision of   (an independent organization) , whose decision will be final.

3. All prizes, as listed, are guaranteed. No substitutions will be made for any prize offered.

5. Customers may cast a ballot for each minimum $5 purchase made in any store. Ballots are available at cash desks and are given to customers when payment for their purchases is made.

6. Only full- or part-time employees in the center are eligible for employee prizes.

7. One prize *only* per family will be awarded.

8. Tax liability on any prize will be the responsibility of the prizewinners.

9. Winners need not be present at the drawing. They will be notified by mail.

10. A list of prizewinners can be mailed after   (date)   to anyone requesting this information. The request must be accompanied by a stamped, self-addressed envelope sent to: (address of Promotion Director).

11. Store employees are not eligible to vote for another employee. First prize is transportation via (airline name) nonstop jet service to (city or country). Land-travel arrangements for 7 nights at a leading hotel (European Plan) courtesy of (travel service). (Ask any store employee about other fabulous prizes.)

IMPORTANT! ADDITIONAL INSTRUCTIONS TO STORE EMPLOYEES:

1. Starting   (date) , all store employees **must wear the enclosed badge in order to be eligible for a prize!**

2. It is permissible to suggest that customers vote for you if they were happy with your service. The more votes that are cast for you, the better your chances are to have your name drawn and to be a winner.

3. When winning entries are drawn, it is possible the ballot may not contain your name, **just your number.** Since we may **not** have a record of names and numbers, it is your responsibility to notify _____, Promotion Director, of your identity so we may present you with your prize if you are a winner.

As soon as the drawing has been completed, we will distribute a list of winning names **or** numbers to all tenants. If your number (but not your name) is on this list, notify the promotion office immediately. Your badge will be the only acceptable proof of identity, so don't lose it or leave it where someone else can pick it up. It could cost you your prize.

4. Ballots may be deposited only at the two official polling booths on the mall. **Be sure to tell your customers where they are located, otherwise they will not be able to vote for you!**

If you have any questions, telephone the Promotion Office. Obviously not everyone can win a prize, but if you really make a great effort during our Courtesy Campaign, everyone benefits—you . . . the customer . . . and Bel Air Shopping City.

PRIZES: EMPLOYEES

1st Prize—Round-trip tickets for two via   (name of airline)   to (city or country).
Land-travel arrangements for 7 nights at a leading hotel (European Plan) courtesy of (travel service).
2nd PRIZE—$100 in Cash
3rd PRIZE—$75 in Cash
BONUS PRIZES—50 awards of $5 each

PRIZES: CUSTOMERS

1st PRIZE—Round-trip tickets for two via   (name of airline) to (city or country).
Land-travel arrangements for 7 nights at a leading hotel (European Plan) courtesy of (travel service).
2nd PRIZE—$100 Merchandise Gift Certificate
3rd PRIZE—$75 Merchandise Gift Certificate
Bonus Prizes—50 - $5 Merchandise Gift Certificates

OFFICIAL COURTESY CAMPAIGN BALLOT

I hereby cast ONE VOTE for Store Employee

(Name) and _____ (Badge Number) _____
for the courteous service rendered me while shopping at

(Store Name) _____

NAME: _____

ADDRESS: _____

CITY: _____ STATE: _____ ZIP _____

I understand this ballot also makes me eligible to win a prize in the Courtesy Campaign drawing to be held 6:00 p.m., Saturday,   (date)   .(All prize awards are subject to the rules printed on the official ballot.)

A VOTE FOR COURTESY PAYS OFF IN FREE TRIPS AND CASH AT BEL AIR SHOPPING CITY DURING THEIR MONTH LONG COURTESY CAMPAIGN.

Every Bel Air Shopping City store employee will be campaigning hard to please you. And they've got good reason—free jet-away vacations for BOTH customers AND employees and great prizes.

Every Bel Air store employee wearing a smiling-face identification badge is an eligible candidate. If you're happy with the service you received while shopping, note the employee's name and badge number. Complete the ballot you will receive with each purchase of $5 or more, and deposit it in one of our polling booths on the mall. This automatically makes YOU eligible to win a prize, too!

Every vote for courtesy means someone has made your shopping day at Bel Air a little more pleasant. Come shop. Come vote. You may win a wonderful prize. Winners will be selected by a drawing at 6:00 p.m., Saturday   (date)

IN STORE DISPLAY MATERIAL

10″ × 15″ two-color, easel-back counter cards   14″ × 22″ window signs

YOU CAN WIN A FREE (city or country) VACATION FOR TWO VIA (name of airline)

OTHER VALUABLE PRIZES, TOO! CAST A VOTE FOR COURTESY DURING THE BEL AIR SHOPPING CITY COURTESY CAMPAIGN
Details in all mall stores

Children's Petting Zoo. This is an easily maneuvered, highly productive attraction that can generate thousands of additional mall visitors. The live exhibit has tremendous appeal to young children who must, of course, be accompanied by their parents or other adults.

The heart of even the crustiest curmudgeon can be warmed by a petting zoo; that is, a variety of tame, domesticated animals that may be safely petted and fed by the "young of all ages." In planning the zoo, timing is important—the zoo should be scheduled when schools are not in session. Because it is an on-going event, it is not necessary to establish a specific schedule of zoo operation. The animal compound is set up in a central area of the mall and supervised by personnel affiliated with the live-animal exhibit.

With its strong and proven universal draw, an accompanying merchandise promotion is not obligatory, although the zoo will add punch and give the promotion balance. For maximum attendance, the "petting zoo" and an accompanying merchandise promotion (if one is planned) must be well publicized. This can be achieved by:

- **"Teaser"** newspaper ads for several days preceding the start of the exhibit.

- Newspaper ads on the day before and day of the zoo opening. These ads should give details about operating hours, zoo location in the mall, and free admission to children accompanied by adults.

- Radio or television spots providing the same information that appears in the newspaper ads (as above).

- Using the cover page of a special merchandise section or a banner at the top of cooperative pages, again giving the essential details. This publicity is based on the assumption that there is an accompanying merchandise promotion.

The judicious selection of traffic-building devices used as primary attractions is essential if tenants are to receive maximum benefits from their assessment dollars. Proper timing, forceful publicity, and advance planning will accomplish this result—and the "petting zoo" can be a star performer.

The high cost special events are designed to accelerate center traffic—with or without the benefit of merchandise advertising and promotion. These devices can enable a center to get more than its share of potential shoppers during normally high-volume periods.

The individual programs detailed in this chapter are examples of exciting, imaginative devices designed to build center traffic. There are many others in use, new programs are devised almost daily. The budget, local preferences, and timing are the factors to be most considered in the selection and development of nonmerchandise promotions that will be most beneficial. Most of all, it is the imagination, creativity, and initiative of the marketing director who ultimately develops the new ideas that make shopping center promotion so exciting and challenging.

Discussion Questions 7

1. Communication is important to successful promotion. Name the various facts merchants should have on hand about all upcoming events.

2. The two basic types of promotions are merchandise and special events. Explain the difference in concept and purpose.

3. The quantity of special events is no substitute for their quality, timing, and implementation. Explain.

4. Name some "do's" and "don'ts" on how to decide on the timing of merchandise events.

5. Merchandise and special events can and should be used jointly in many instances. Explain and give some examples.

6. Describe the three categories of traffic-building events.

7. While the budget dictates expenditures, creativity is an important commodity. Discuss "dollar-stretching" techniques the marketing/promotion director can use.

8. Plan a coordinated merchandising and special event promotion. Detail the steps you would take to put the program into operation.

8

CALENDAR OF MERCHANDISE PROMOTIONS

In the preceding chapter, we examined some of the promotional campaigns that can be effected after the 30-day postopening period. Those promotions can be used to supplement merchandise events, although many could function as self-generating traffic producers, connected to the merchandise promotions only in a peripheral sense.

In this chapter, we turn to this most important aspect of shopping center promotion—the merchandise events. The proposals presented in this chapter encompass an entire year of merchandising events. They can be adapted to any budget, altered to take into account a variety of climatic conditions, and tailored to the physical characteristics of a particular center. In other words, it is a basic structure on which you can build your own promotion program.

For ease of presentation, we've created the mythical shopping center mentioned previously, Bel Air Shopping City, which from time to time is referred to in terms of specific promotion plans. Full facts about this center appear elsewhere, but let's assume it is in an enclosed mall located in Asheville, North Carolina.

SEASONAL AND SPECIAL-OCCASION PROMOTIONS

After Christmas or January Clearance. Begin this event immediately after Christmas or as soon as a majority of the merchant-tenants are prepared for it. The timing is excellent because customer traffic continues strong during the Christmas-to-New Year week, fueled by exchanges of Christmas gifts and the traditional after-Christmas sale events.

The success of this clearance event depends on full centerwide participation in the merchandising effort, using cooperative advertising with a common "handle" or theme and operating as a single entity instead of as individual merchants.

Because of the natural traffic flow mentioned above, merchandising will make the greater contribution—which may, if desired, be supplemented by a nonmerchandise event ("Low-Budget Promotional Events" are applicable here; see Chapter 7). Because the Christmas decor remains in the center and in the individual stores through the New Year, an event may not be necessary.

President's Days Sales. Washington's and Lincoln's Birthdays, during February, have become extremely strong, "low-end" sale periods. They have been further strengthened by a congressionally mandated change in the celebration of Washington's Birthday from February 22 to the third Monday of February, providing a long weekend holiday when schools, banks, and most offices close.

Because of this date change many shopping centers have combined Lincoln's and Washington's birthdays into a single "Presidents' Days" promotion, thus creating an event of approximately one week's duration. Other areas handle these natural sale periods individually as single- or multi-day promotions, while still others, particularly in those states where Lincoln's Birthday is not a legal holiday, run Washington's Birthday sales only.

Both of these holidays coincide with normally low-volume periods that require aggressive efforts to stimulate traffic and sales. In addition, fashion merchants must clear remaining stocks of the past season's merchandise; similarly, department stores and appliance stores seek to liquidate cold-weather "hard goods," while they begin to promote warm-weather appliances, home improvement items, garden equipment, and so forth. For these reasons, the scheduling of merchandise promotions during these two holidays is necessary and advisable. The timing, duration, and whether they are planned as a single event starting on Lincoln's Birthday and continuing through Washington's Birthday depends on the individual center, on available merchandise of the types described, and, of course, on whether Lincoln's Birthday is a legal holiday.

Here are simple guidelines to follow:

• If Lincoln's Birthday is a legal holiday, serious consideration should be given to the scheduling of a single-event "Presidents' Birthday Sale" to extend through Washington's Birthday.

• If available merchandise of the types mentioned is inadequate, individual Lincoln's and Washington's Birthday events should be held and can be limited to one or two days each.

• If Lincoln's Birthday is *not* celebrated in your area, plan a Washington's Birthday event of one, two, or three days.

Regardless of the course followed, the event(s) should be promoted to the maximum degree permitted by the budget. Use the most effective means of promotion—the special section or cooperative pages, and radio and/or television spots.

Although the budget will dictate the depth and volume of the effort, a major consideration must also be the duration of the event and whether Lincoln's and Washington's Birthdays will be celebrated jointly as "Presidents' Sale Days" or individually. Obviously, a one-day event does not deserve the same expenditure as week-long promotions.

Thus, the merchandise advertising for a one-day event can be handled on double-page spreads of cooperative pages with promotional banners instead of a special section with a cover page, normally used for a promotion of longer duration. Radio and television spots would similarly require a smaller expenditure for a shorter event, with maximum exposure during the afternoon and evening preceding the morning the sale begins. Longer promotions should use airborne media starting earlier the preceding day and continuing through the morning of the final event-day. Properly exploited, "Presidents' Sale Days," promoted individually or in combination, can produce an extremely heavy flow of customer traffic by virtue of the merchandising effort and approach. For these reasons, exhibits, shows, or similar activities are generally unnecessary. However, if the merchants desire an attraction, choose one from the low-budget or no-budget events.

After Easter Clearance. The post-Easter clearance is not just another sale event, but a major clearance operation. Accordingly, this event becomes particularly urgent for every store involved with the sale of fashion: department stores, specialty shops for both women and men, boutiques, children's shops, and shoe stores. Other merchants can and should join the sale event by offering slow-moving or stagnant merchandise at sale prices.

A strong sale event, timed to start immediately after Easter, will clear stocks of merchandise before summer buying begins, while increasing volume during the normally inactive days that follow Easter. To be successful, the event requires the participation of a large majority of the merchants, a special section, and radio and television spots as the budget allows. The nature of this event generally makes necessary an accompanying traffic-building device that should be relatively strong and that will in itself be responsible for the visits of substantial numbers of shoppers to the center. It is recommended that a choice be made from those listed under "Moderate-Cost Promotional Events" in Chapter 7.

The retail doldrums inevitably follow Christmas. The remaining winter months are slow seasons for most merchants. To stimulate traffic and sales, consider launching a strong

Lincoln's-Washington's day sales campaign. These eye-catching illustrations might give you an idea for a special section or an institutional ad.

Pre-Vacation Promotion. Plan this event for early June to coincide with the purchase of "easy-living" merchandise. Both the theme and the timing permit participation by all tenants, especially the department stores, women's and men's specialty shops, boutiques, children's stores, and sporting goods merchants.

This should be a three-day-weekend event, with all participants using the "pre-vacation" theme and offering timely merchandise during the period. Full participation will strengthen the presentation, thus giving shoppers a wider choice of items for vacations and for summer leisure activities, which are still ahead. It can be an important volume-producer and should be supported by a special merchandise section. The section's cover page should provide pertinent details including the theme and the days of the event. Because there are many shows, exhibits, and programs that do coordinate well with the "pre-vacation" theme, choose an accompanying nonmerchandise event.

An excellent choice would be "Vacation Week," which is described in detail under "Moderate-Cost Promotional Events" in Chapter 7. Announcement of "Vacation Week" should also be included on the cover page of the special section together with the details of the merchandise promotion. Merchandise offerings will be at regular prices, although some merchants may advertise sale events. This well-aligned tandem operation deserves the support of all merchants, large and small alike, and will be productive.

July Summer Clearance. This is a "must" merchandising extravaganza for every Bel Air Shopping City tenant. This is the beginning of the end of the summer season; therefore, all merchants can and should participate in the effort to clear away stocks of warm-weather merchandise. A potpourri of items would be included: women's, men's, and children's fashions; and hard goods, such as air conditioners, fans, and garden equipment.

The department stores would benefit greatly from a strong event because they stock almost every category of merchandise that would be on sale. They should be consulted before the dates are firmly set and, if at all possible, the

scheduling adjusted to meet their needs. Faster-than-usual clearance of seasonal merchandise will avoid costly additional markdowns that would be taken subsequently, and will provide the space for new-season inventories.

Obviously, the success of this effort will depend on full merchant participation in the promotional activities. Include a tabloid-sized special section in which a majority of the merchants and the anchor stores are well represented. A cover lead-page would "scream" the details: theme, sale days, as well as opening and closing store hours and the specifics of an appropriate traffic-building device. In Chapter 7, are many supplements to merchandise promotions. Select one from the moderate cost list, or improvise an event with local appeal that will pull additional shoppers to the center. A well-balanced program can generate a heavy flow of customer traffic because of the twin approach: merchandise combined with an exciting nonmerchandise event.

August Sidewalk Sale. A great end-of-summer event, this is an excellent promotion for both enclosed and open malls. Schedule the sale for a one-, two-, or three-day period at the very beginning of August.

There are advantages to this selection of date and the type of sale:

• Final markdowns on summer merchandise will normally have been taken during the first week of August, because only a limited selling period for summer merchandise remains at that point.

• While the selections may be limited, the prices must be very attractive because the end of the summer season is approaching. Together, the suggested timing and the great savings will create a most successful event.

• Booths, tables, and racks outside the stores project a real carnival air, and when combined with the sale prices will induce many customers to buy more readily. Many centers own such equipment and allocate it to tenants based on their square foot area or requests. If equipment is not readily available, it can be rented, with the cost absorbed by the mer-

In mid-spring and again in mid-summer, merchants want to clear stocks to make room for incoming merchandise for the next season. A coordinated advertising-promotion campaign can give them an all-important boost. At the top are two special section cover ideas for spring and summer clearances.

Labor Day and the back-to-school season also mark a strong regular-priced selling period. Immediately following this merchandise season, however, merchants must make room for winter and Christmas offerings. The two bottom covers might give you ideas about how to help merchants achieve their goals.

chants association or promotion fund. If the budget does not provide for this expense, each participating merchant can be charged for the use of the equipment.

• Another important benefit of the increased customer traffic on the mall is the overflow of "sidewalk sale" shoppers into store interiors. The obvious advantage of this in-store customer shopping is the exposure of new season merchandise to customers.

Additional on-the-mall activity is unnecessary since the "sidewalk sale" held on the mall and another "happening" would cause confusion and detract from the pull of the major merchandise event. If merchants wish to use a nonmerchandising supplement, it should be chosen from the low-budget promotional ideas in the preceding chapter, but it should be held in the auditorium to avoid taking up space in the common areas.

Advertising and promotion for a "sidewalk sale" should be as extensive as the budget permits. A special tabloid section or cooperative pages are necessary to publicity, and the cover page of the section or the banner across the cooperative pages should tell the story of what can be a most productive event. Radio and/or television exposure is desirable as a supplement to the print media and should be used in spot announcements to the degree permitted by merchants association funds.

Fall Festival of Values. Starting in late August and up to school openings, much of the buying emphasis is on back-to-school and campus and career merchandise. After that, traffic and buying tapers off for several weeks until there is a resurgence of buying in anticipation of the fall and winter seasons ahead.

A Fall Festival of Values should be timed for the period almost immediately after school openings and before the start of active shopping for fall and winter items. This event helps to bridge the gap during a lull in customer activity. Shoppers would find the best of two worlds: the opportunity to purchase some back-to-school and campus fashions at reduced prices—because of post-back-to-school markdowns—and to buy fashions needed for fall and winter from the most complete stocks.

The scheduling of a pre-Back-to-School, Campus and Career merchandising event is usually not advisable, since at that time the traffic pattern in the center would normally be active, and people need not be enticed to buy. Therefore, a post-Back-to-School event is often more productive.

Although the Fall Festival of Values promotion is not an absolute must, it is important for the reasons given and is best handled as follows:

• Produce a special section in which—we hope—merchants, including the anchor stores, will advertise.

• Use the cover page to exploit the merchandise event and an accompanying traffic-building event.

• Publicize the events with radio and/or television spots as permitted by the budget.

• Use a nonmerchandise traffic-builder as a supplement and follow the guidelines in the preceding chapter (a moderate-cost or high-cost event would be chosen for this effort).

Anniversary Celebration. This celebration can be an important and productive sale event. The budget should provide adequate funds for its promotion, which is timed to coincide with the center's anniversary date, or thereabouts.

Bel Air Shopping City opened on Thursday, October 5th. Columbus Day, which is a school holiday in many areas and generally a strong retail day, is the second Monday of October. We have then a strong combination of events that provide excellent timing for an Anniversary Sale.

Retailers generally frown on sale events that are longer than three or four days and that do not include a weekend. Considering this, the Anniversary Sale event would be most effective for Thursday, Friday, and Saturday. If Sunday is a normal shopping day, and Monday a holiday, the anniversary sale is then combined with Columbus Day, thus creating a single strong event from two normally powerful sale periods.

Timing that permits Bel Air merchants a

weekend promotion as well as Monday, Columbus Day, will be ideal because many people have a holiday on Columbus Day. Plan the Anniversary Celebration well in advance. Develop a special section, preferably tabloid-size, in which a great majority of the merchants, including anchor stores, will advertise their own sale items. A dynamic cover page, exploiting both the Anniversary Sale and Columbus Day, would provide the details, including sale dates and the specifics on a major traffic-building event.

The print media provides a vehicle for individual merchandise advertising, which is unified by the cover page and is a physical reminder for customers. Radio and/or television spots add excitement and provide specifics: place, days of sale, details of the companion nonmerchandise events, and so on. Individual merchants may, of course, use radio and TV at their own expense, concurrently with the institutional spot announcements, to promote their own merchandise. The Anniversary Celebration deserves the greatest possible exposure, since it is a good way of advertising the center and its history, and since it will demand a major companion nonmerchandise event. Chapter 7 provides a choice of exciting ideas for this effort, or you may develop one specifically for the occasion that creates the pull the event deserves. Publicize the event on the cover page of the special section, using an attention-getting motif for this purpose.

The importance of the Anniversary Celebration cannot be overemphasized. The degree of its success is strongly influenced by factors already mentioned: timing, merchant participation, radio and television, as well as the appeal of the companion nonmerchandise event. While the combination of an anniversary and Columbus Day is an ideal tandem that offers opportunity to further the importance of Bel Air Shopping City as an integral part of the community, all centers have their own dates and associations that can be exploited, and the principles presented here apply everywhere.

Election Day Sale. This is a traditionally strong shopping day strengthened further by the fact that schools are closed. Most merchants capitalize on the increased traffic flow and volume potential with timely merchandise promotions.

Election day is a highly productive time for retailers who recognize the importance of coordinating their promotional activities with the holiday. If individual merchants benefit substantially from their own aggressive efforts, clearly a shopping center must derive far greater results with a unified common presentation. The formula for the best possible results is strongly dependent on the degree of emphasis placed on the occasion and the cooperation of tenants in the endeavor. A unified approach should include these steps:

• Develop a special merchandise section fronted with a cover page that provides the details of the event, including the Election Day theme, the sale days, and any device relating to Election Day that would further build traffic. If this is a one-day sale only, cooperative pages would be effective, with equal-size boxes and banners explaining the event.

• Use a common merchandising approach in which all merchants will offer some sale items that are traditional for Election Day.

• Schedule radio and/or television spots that announce the Election Day events, both merchandise and nonmerchandise, at the center.

An exciting traffic-building device for Election Day could feature a computer screen centrally located in one or two areas of the mall to convey the latest election results periodically. By offering this service a center would accomplish two objectives: bring customers out of their homes and further its image as an integral part of the community.

An Election Day Sale can be of one or two days duration: Tuesday, Election Day, only, or Monday and Tuesday. A two-day event would provide the opportunity to insert the special section in the Sunday newspaper, which is the most widely read, and still provide a sale event on Election day. A one-day-only Election Day promotion would concentrate all of the shopping into Tuesday, making it a much stronger day than it would be if two sale days were involved. As a general guideline, the two-day event, with its advantage of Sunday advertising and a school holiday on Election Day, is normally the stronger of the two alternatives.

Veterans' Day Sale. Although congressionally designated as the fourth Monday in October, Veterans' Day has been returned to its original November 11 date in most states. This is a traditionally strong retail period, generally fueled by a sale accompanied by an on-the-mall nonmerchandise event. A Veterans' Day Sale, too, should be promoted with a special tabloid section or a series of facing cooperative pages with banners describing the event, while providing other necessary details. The duration of the sale would depend on when Veterans' Day is observed: if on a Monday, the advertising would appear on Sunday for a one- or two-day, Monday and/or Tuesday, sale. If the holiday is on Tuesday or Wednesday, a one- or two-day promotion is in order and, if it falls on Thursday or Friday, run a two- or three-day sale event.

Depending on the availability of funds in the merchants association budget, the print advertising should be supplemented with the usual radio and/or television spots that would provide specifics of the event. Many centers have on-going spots in either or both of the electronic media and the usual announcements should, of course, promote Veterans' Day, to be strengthened with additional spots as the budget permits.

The promotions immediately preceding Election Day and the Veterans' Day sale have the potential for greater-than-normal customer traffic, which translates into large volume. The center must, therefore, promote both holidays to the fullest extent possible. If special sections are not possible, use facing cooperative pages with banners, and limit the expenditure for supplementary nonmerchandise events. In any circumstances, participate in both or be resigned to the loss of volume to your competition.

SPOT PROMOTIONS

The calendar of merchandise events should include one-day "spot" promotions designed to build a heavy customer traffic that should naturally result in substantial volume increases. But the word "naturally" is used advisedly, because the suggested events that follow will bring the necessary traffic to increase volume; those merchants who participate in the cooperative advertising and offer the best values will benefit most.

The most consistently effective one-day spot promotions are:

Moonlite or Midnite Sales. These events are geared for high traffic and high volume within a short time span. This may be a four- to six-hour sale starting at 6 or 7 p.m. and ending between 10 p.m. and midnight. As an alternative, merchants can offer special bargains during half-hour periods at various times during the evenings.

Merchants may wish to close their stores for an hour immediately preceding the sales to prepare the merchandise, signs, floor alignment, and so on. The merchandise offered is end-of-season, reduced to ridiculously low prices and available in limited quantities only. To keep the event honest, this fact is mentioned in the advertising, which should include "Limited Quantities, While They Last," in the banner.

Merchandise action as described above generates customer excitement, which produces greater-than-normal traffic and ultimately results in the sale of substantial quantities of the current season's regularly priced items.

Ladies Day at Bel Air Shopping City. This one-day event offers the best of two worlds: a means to increased volume and a great builder of community good will. However, it can be utilized only in centers with a movie theater on the premises. The mechanics of this promotion are relatively simple and it is inexpensive as well.

Offer a movie to *Ladies Only*, timed to start when the center opens in the morning and to end at or shortly before noon. The performance will be free to the viewers, or for a very minimal charge. The merchants association or promotion fund would subsidize the expense for the operators of the theater. The movie would be scheduled for the least active day of the week on a monthly, semimonthly, or weekly basis.

The event must be publicized to the degree permitted by the merchants association budget, using teaser newspaper announcements, radio or television spots, and cooperative merchandise advertising with banner headlines. The items advertised would be "Ladies Day Specials," and slides on the movie screen can be used to promote them further. Restaurants or coffee shops in Bel Air Shopping City would offer a "Ladies Day Luncheon Special," and these menus could also be publicized on the movie screen. Merchants would time their "Ladies Day Specials" to start immediately after the movie ends and continue for the balance of that day.

Ladies Days have proven themselves. They are highly productive, low-budget events that transform low-volume days into active ones and at the same time build good will in a prime shoppers group.

Breakfast Specials. Here is another unique event designed to increase the traffic flow during a morning or on a day that is normally weak. The operation is relatively simple and the cost minimal.

Set up one or more canteens in several areas of the mall offering free danish pastry or donuts and coffee to adults. Each canteen should bear a sign to publicize the free refreshments and the specials being offered by center merchants.

The mini-breakfasts should be made available approximately 30 minutes before the normal opening hour, and continue being served for 30 minutes after the center usually opens. The cost is usually borne by the merchants association or promotion fund, and food is purchased from a coffee shop on the mall at substantially reduced prices. In some instances, the coffee shop will donate the food in exchange for publicity and good will.

Because the objective is more shoppers at an early hour, the free breakfasts must be publicized and merchants should offer specials for that morning or for the entire day. A series of facing pages divided into boxes and headed with a banner can promote both the mini-breakfasts and the special merchandise offered. It is recommended that this event be repeated on the same day every week until volume improves sufficiently to warrant its discontinuance. Consistent participation by a majority of the merchants, including the department stores, and honest values in sufficient quantities to meet customer requests are the important factors in making the event successful.

COOPERATIVE ADVERTISING FOR SPECIFIC ONE-DAY EVENTS

The success and great popularity of the centers that remain open on legal holidays—particularly Memorial Day and Labor Day—have caused these holidays to become strong retail days.

While both holidays are observed on a Monday, at the start of a new season, some shopping centers create two- or three-day events. This spreads the volume over a longer span during periods that are normally productive, and the events usually do not require extra stimulus. But if the promotion is for the holiday alone (one day only), the pull of sale advertising is required to bring in potential shoppers who could otherwise easily be diverted to different activities.

An event of more than one day's duration is most effectively promoted with a special section. A one-day event can be publicized with bannered facing pages of cooperative boxes. The dollar return from a one-day event does not normally justify the cost of special-section advertising, and this factor could decrease the extent of merchant participation.

For these reasons, and because both holidays occur at the beginning of a season, with Memorial Day marking the start of summer and Labor Day the beginning of fall, Bel Air Shopping City opted to limit the necessary sale event to the one day of the holiday alone. This curtailing action attracts more customers to the shopping center, limits the cost of markdowns on the sale items, and reduces both the advertising and publicity expense. Publicity would be handled by radio spots during the preceding day and merchandise advertising would be in the form of box ads on facing pages, with banners providing the details.

The sale event, merchandise advertising, and publicity are absolutely essential if merchants are to derive the maximum benefit from these holiday openings and remain competitive.

Arts to Zoo
Guide to Promotion Events

If you want to attract these shoppers, consider these ideas:

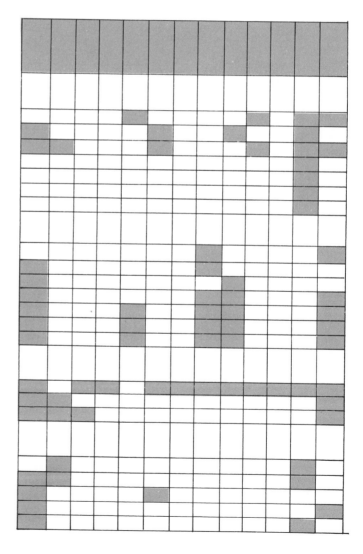

	Adults	Career People	Culture Buffs	Homeowners	Homemakers	Men	Nature Lovers	Parents	Senior Citizens	Singles	Sports Fans	Working Women	Youth
ARTS (exhibits, local talent, collections, demonstrations, instructions, seminars, workshops, contests, concerts, performances)	■	■	■	■	■	■	■	■	■	■	■	■	■
BEAUTY													
beauty-on-the-go					■					■		■	
diet	■				■					■		■	■
exercise	■				■					■		■	■
hair-dos/don'ts													
make-overs													
make-up													
skin care												■	
BENEFITS													
high school—class trip							■						■
scholarship fund/building fund	■												
local charity—historical society	■							■	■				
library/religious orgs./orphanage	■			■				■					
national charity—cancer society	■						■					■	
united fund/muscular dystrophy	■												
telethon tie-in													
BOOKS													
book fair	■	■	■	■	■								■
how to get published	■	■											
meet local/touring authors	■		■									■	
CAREERS													
careers for women		■										■	
job exchange													
military opportunities						■							
preparation/training/education												■	
second careers	■										■	■	

CELEBRITIES

CINEMA
cartoons
disney
home movie festival
clinic/equipment show
silents
stars

COMMUNICATIONS
satellite
telephone

CRAFTS
(workshops, exhibits, demonstrations, sales, auctions)
basket weaving
batik
bread-dough art
candlemaking
ceramics
crochet
decoupage
embroidery
ethnic crafts
flower arranging
glass cutting/blowing
historic/old time
holiday crafts
jewelry
knitting
leather tooling
macramé
needlepoint
pottery
sewing
silk flowers
silkscreen
tailoring
tie-dying
weaving

DANCE
ballet-local/touring companies
disco
ethnic

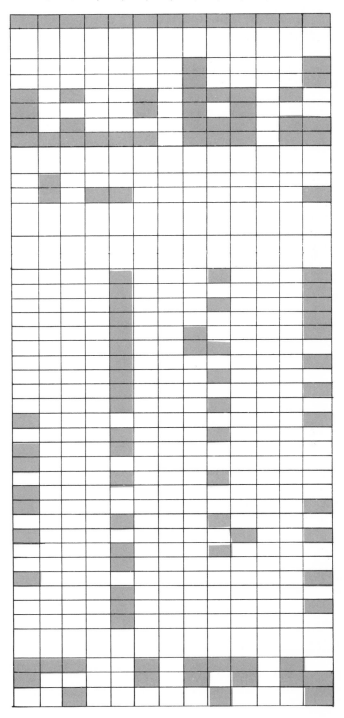

	Adults	Career People	Culture Buffs	Homeowners	Homemakers	Men	Nature Lovers	Parents	Senior Citizens	Singles	Sports Fans	Working Women	Youth
CELEBRITIES	■	■	■	■	■	■	■	■	■	■	■	■	■
cartoons							■						■
disney													
home movie festival	■		■			■		■				■	
clinic/equipment show	■					■				■		■	
silents	■		■				■				■	■	
stars	■	■		■		■		■		■	■		
satellite		■											
telephone		■	■										
basket weaving				■					■				■
batik				■									■
bread-dough art				■					■				■
candlemaking				■									■
ceramics				■				■					
crochet				■					■				
decoupage				■									
embroidery				■					■				
ethnic crafts				■									
flower arranging				■					■				
glass cutting/blowing	■			■									
historic/old time	■												
holiday crafts	■			■									
jewelry				■					■				
knitting				■						■			
leather tooling	■												
macramé				■									■
needlepoint	■								■				
pottery	■									■			■
sewing				■					■				
silk flowers				■									
silkscreen	■			■									■
tailoring				■									
tie-dying				■									
weaving													
ballet-local/touring companies	■		■		■		■				■		■
disco	■									■			■
ethnic			■					■					■

	Adults	Career People	Culture Buffs	Homeowners	Homemakers	Men	Nature Lovers	Parents	Senior Citizens	Singles	Sports Fans	Working Women	Youth
folk			■						■				■
historical									■				■
marathon										■			■
square dance													
tap													

DOLLS

	Adults	Career People	Culture Buffs	Homeowners	Homemakers	Men	Nature Lovers	Parents	Senior Citizens	Singles	Sports Fans	Working Women	Youth
collections													■
doll hospital													
ethnic													■
handmade													
historical			■					■					

DRAWING/PAINTING SCULPTURE

	Adults	Career People	Culture Buffs	Homeowners	Homemakers	Men	Nature Lovers	Parents	Senior Citizens	Singles	Sports Fans	Working Women	Youth
charcoal	■		■					■					■
pastel	■		■					■					■
pen & ink	■		■					■					■
pencil	■		■					■					■
oil painting	■							■					
watercolor	■							■					
bronze	■							■					
clay	■							■					
stone	■							■					

EDUCATION

	Adults	Career People	Culture Buffs	Homeowners	Homemakers	Men	Nature Lovers	Parents	Senior Citizens	Singles	Sports Fans	Working Women	Youth
career preparation	■	■				■		■	■		■		
college/trade school	■	■						■	■		■		
life enrichment studies	■	■							■				
meet the school board	■	■						■					
methods							■	■					
options	■						■	■	■				
salute to schools/teachers													
science fair													
spelling bee													

FASHION

	Adults	Career People	Culture Buffs	Homeowners	Homemakers	Men	Nature Lovers	Parents	Senior Citizens	Singles	Sports Fans	Working Women	Youth
bridal										■		■	
campus	■												■
children								■					■
designers		■											
disco fashion	■									■			■
foreign costume			■							■			■
historic													
local designers													
men						■							
school clothes	■			■									■

	Adults	Career People	Culture Buffs	Homeowners	Homemakers	Men	Nature Lovers	Parents	Senior Citizens	Singles	Sports Fans	Working Women	Youth
self-made				■									
sports fashion	■					■					■		■
women	■								■	■		■	

FOOD

	Adults	Career People	Culture Buffs	Homeowners	Homemakers	Men	Nature Lovers	Parents	Senior Citizens	Singles	Sports Fans	Working Women	Youth
cook-off				■						■			
ethnic—chinese/italian/japanese etc.	■			■				■		■			
regional/u.s.	■	■		■									
haute cuisine	■			■			■			■			
homegrown food/canning/processing	■			■			■	■					
preservation/jams/jellies				■									
how to use food processors	■			■								■	
cook with a wok/cook with a blender	■			■						■			
local restaurant sampler/demonstrations				■					■	■			
recipe exchange				■	■			■					
special diets—low sodium/high protein-health food/vegetarian	■			■			■		■			■	

GAMES PEOPLE PLAY

	Adults	Career People	Culture Buffs	Homeowners	Homemakers	Men	Nature Lovers	Parents	Senior Citizens	Singles	Sports Fans	Working Women	Youth
(tournaments, demonstrations)													
backgammon	■					■		■	■	■	■		■
bridge	■					■		■	■				
checkers	■												■
chess	■					■				■			■
monopoly	■							■					■

GARDENING

	Adults	Career People	Culture Buffs	Homeowners	Homemakers	Men	Nature Lovers	Parents	Senior Citizens	Singles	Sports Fans	Working Women	Youth
flowers	■		■	■			■	■				■	
fruits and vegetables	■		■	■			■	■					
furniture	■												
landscaping	■		■	■				■					
lawn care clinic	■		■	■									
problems/solutions clinic	■		■	■									

GOVERNMENT

	Adults	Career People	Culture Buffs	Homeowners	Homemakers	Men	Nature Lovers	Parents	Senior Citizens	Singles	Sports Fans	Working Women	Youth
(county/federal/local/state)													
complaint booth	■	■		■		■				■			
how it runs	■		■										■
services	■		■						■				

HEALTH

	Adults	Career People	Culture Buffs	Homeowners	Homemakers	Men	Nature Lovers	Parents	Senior Citizens	Singles	Sports Fans	Working Women	Youth
arthritis	■								■				
blood pressure tests													
cancer association	■						■						■
children	■						■	■					
county medical assn.	■												

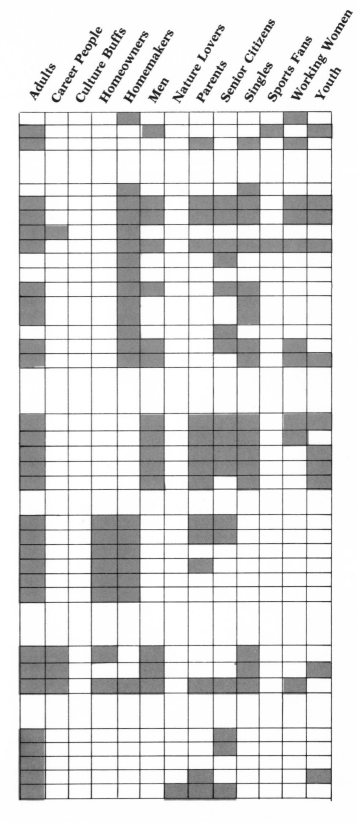

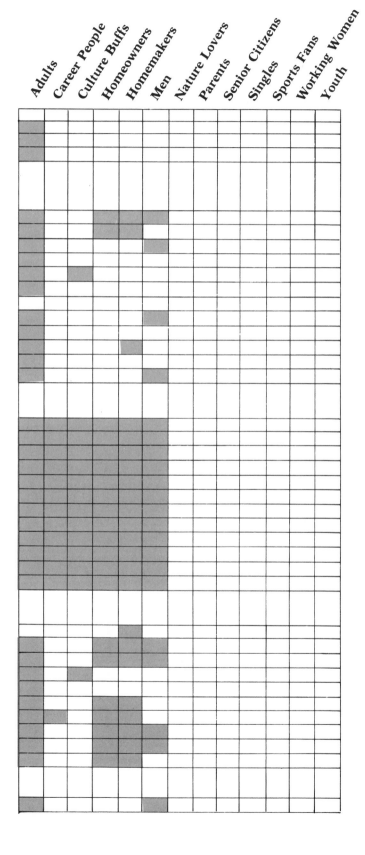

	Adults	Career People	Culture Buffs	Homeowners	Homemakers	Men	Nature Lovers	Parents	Senior Citizens	Singles	Sports Fans	Working Women	Youth
expectant mothers													
mental health assn.													
older people	X												
x-ray clinic													
HOBBIES													
(collections)													
antiques	X												
art			X	X									
automobiles						X							
autographs													
books—first editions/old/comic	X	X											
bottles													
bubble gum cards													
coins	X					X							
collections													
glass	X			X									
memorabilia													
stamps	X					X							
HOLIDAYS													
christmas	X	X	X	X	X	X							
columbus day	X	X	X	X	X	X							
easter	X	X	X	X	X	X							
fourth of july	X	X	X	X	X	X							
hanukkah	X	X	X	X	X	X							
labor day	X	X	X	X	X	X							
leap year	X	X	X	X	X	X							
memorial day	X	X	X	X	X	X							
new year's day	X	X	X	X	X	X							
passover	X	X	X	X	X	X							
thanksgiving	X	X	X	X	X	X							
valentine's day	X	X	X	X	X	X							
HOME													
carpentry for women					X								
energy-saving techniques	X			X	X								
furniture repair	X			X									
historic homes	X		X										
home of the future	X												
interior decorating advice	X			X	X								
model home/rooms	X	X		X	X								
remodeling	X			X	X	X							
safety	X			X	X								
winterizing/summerizing	X			X									
LOCAL INTEREST													
ethnic groups	X					X							

first citizens
history
indians
industry
old times

MONEY

investment clinic
money management seminar
taxes

MUSIC

band—high school
barbershop quartet
chamber music group
disco
glee club
historic instruments
jazz/swing
musical instruments exposition
opera—local/touring companies
sing-alongs
singers
symphony-local/touring/youth
"what's a symphony?" seminar

ORGANIZATIONS

churches/synagogues
d.a.r.
elks
garden club
kiwanis
knights of columbus
lions
masons
optimists
rotary
scouts
tall cedars

PHOTOGRAPHY

equipment exposition
historic
how to take better pictures
local talent

PUBLIC ISSUES

better business bureau

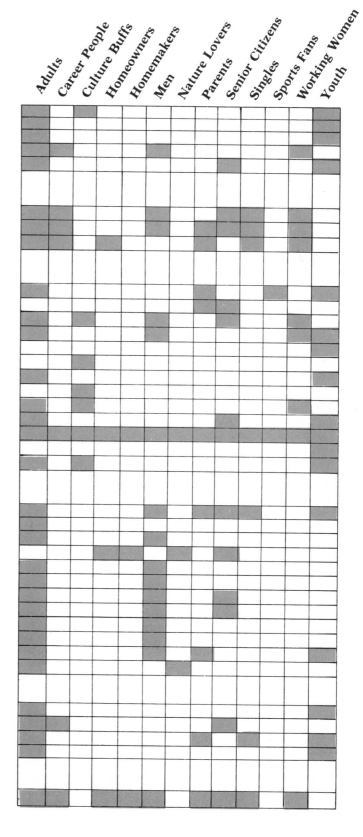

clean air
consumerism
energy
environment
military
nuclear development, pros/cons
politics
schools
transportation
wildlife preservation

SCIENCE
agricultural science
astronomy
botany
ecology
marine biology
NASA lunar module
power/electric company
science fair
space

SEASONS (all four of them)

SORT-OF-SCIENCE
astrology
psychic phenomena
U.F.O. s

SPORTS
demonstrations/competitions/clinics
/local Olympics/Olympics
benefit/salute to
teams/equipment shows)
archery
baseball
basketball
boating
bowling
boxing
canoeing
current/old time
cycling
diving
fencing
flying
football
frisbee

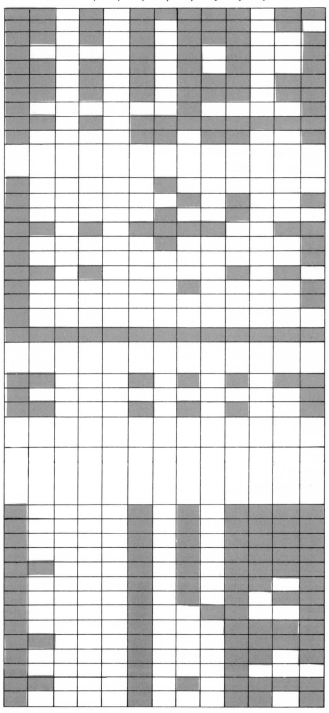

Columns: Adults, Career People, Culture Buffs, Homeowners, Homemakers, Men, Nature Lovers, Parents, Senior Citizens, Singles, Sports Fans, Working Women, Youth

golf
gymnastics
hang-gliding
hockey
hunting
jogging
little league
ping pong
raquetball
sailing
skateboarding
skating—ice/roller
skiing—downhill/cross-country
soccer
squash
swimming
tennis
track & field
wrestling

THEATER

how to break into show biz
local/touring companies
puppets

TRANSPORTATION

airplanes
antique carriages
automobiles—antique/future/new
balloons
bicycles—race/clinic/safety
boats
mass transit
parachute
railroads
unicycle

TRAVEL

canada
featured states
local interest
overseas
u.s.a.

VETERANS

history
local heroes/old timers
salute to vets

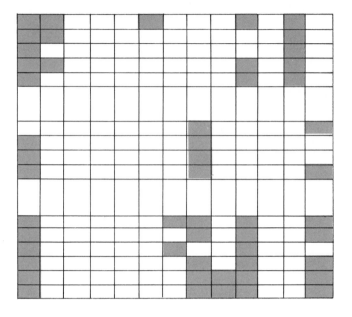

WOMEN

battle of the sexes
career possibilities
new interests
office fashions
sports

YOUTH

fashions
fund raisers
parent/teacher/youth discussion
projects

ZOOS

animals—wild/farm
circus
endangered species
horse show
pet show
pet care clinic

Reprinted courtesy of the Newspaper
  Advertising Bureau

Column headers: Adults · Career People · Culture Buffs · Homeowners · Homemakers · Men · Nature Lovers · Parents · Senior Citizens · Singles · Sports Fans · Working Women · Youth

Discussion Questions 8

1. Ten merchandise promotions are scheduled and presented in the chapter. Assuming the budget can fund only seven, which three can be most easily deleted? Why?

2. Note that most merchandise events are scheduled for natural clearance (or sale) periods. What are the reasons and advantages?

3. Lincoln's and Washington's birthday sale events can be promoted singly or as a combined event. What determines the scheduling?

4. Why is a sale event at Washington's birthday important?

5. Summer clearance events, traditionally starting July 5th in past years, are now beginning during the third and fourth weeks of June. What factors have contributed to this acceleration in the timing?

6. Why are Election, Columbus, and Veterans days important retail days?

7. Spot promotions have a role in the events schedule of every shopping center. Name some of them and discuss their purpose.

8. Can institutional advertising be used to enhance merchandise promotions? If so, why and how?

9

FINAL DO'S AND DONT'S

In conclusion, it seems advisable to summarize and emphasize the actions that make the strongest contribution to a successful shopping center promotion program, as well as those to be avoided because of their detrimental effect:

• **DO** plan and implement the preopening publicity at least six months before the scheduled opening date.

• **DON'T** expect spur-of-the-moment frenetic publicity efforts to accomplish the same results as a planned program.

• **DO** have a working merchants association at least three months in advance of the opening. If the center will operate under the promotion fund concept, the owner-developer should appoint the marketing director, and a merchant steering committee to be in operation at least three months before the grand opening.

• **DON'T** attempt to handle the preopening decisions without either a merchants association or a marketing director and steering committee.

• **DO** develop the preopening and Grand Opening promotional programs well in advance, and in time for presentation to the first general membership meeting.

• **DON'T** permit the preopening and Grand Opening budgets and schedules to be the result of arbitrary decisions by the owner-developer and/or the promotion agency.

• **DO** project subsequent budgets and promotions well in advance, to be approved by the general membership, the board of directors, or the steering committees, as stipulated by lease.

• **DON'T** expect full cooperation and participation unless tenants and/or their board of directors or representatives are given the opportunity to review and accept or recommend modifications of the programs.

• **DO** budget sufficient funds for merchandise promotions timed to generate additional customer traffic when it is most needed.

• **DON'T** overbudget funds for nonmerchandise events if it limits expenditures for merchandise promotions.

• **DO** make the responsibility for adequate participation in merchandise events a function of the marketing director or agency.

• **DON'T** delegate this important role to representatives of any publication.

• **DO** use minimum-cost traffic-builders with major merchandising events.

• **DON'T** employ high-budget devices when the merchandising effort itself may draw a crowd to the center.

• **DO** make every effort to "woo" the community before the center has opened, and thereafter on a continuing basis.

• **DON'T** underestimate the importance of good-will events that must be used to create the center's image.

• **DO** establish and maintain strong lines of communication with all tenants at both the local and headquarters levels.

• **DON'T** expect cooperation unless instructions are clear, concise, and complete, and given with sufficient time to take the necessary action.

The exhibits that follow in the appendixes have been selected after intensive examination and review of many promotional tools. They are presented as the visual demonstration of many of the most salient lessons to be learned from this book. Most have been referred to in the text; it is hoped they will have been studied as the reader went along, to gain the fullest appreciation of how to best use them. In any case, they serve as a ready review and reminder, and as a continuing source of information on the most knowledgeable and practical methods used to handle the many problems of shopping center promotion.

GLOSSARY

Audience: people who comprise the primary and secondary market areas.

Account Executive: supervises client use of print and electronic media as advertising agency representative.

Agate Lines: newspaper advertising unit of measurement; an agate line is one column wide by one-fourteenth of an inch deep.

Anchor Store: major department store branch in a shopping center.

Banner Heading: print media term; positioned across the top of box ad page(s) listing theme, length of event, and other pertinent details.

Box Ads: print media term; generally uniform in size, grouped together under a banner heading promoting a cooperative center event.

Bulk Rate Contract: reduced advertising rate based upon annual linage used.

Camera Ready: print media term; a finished, reproducible typeset paste-up of an ad.

Campaign: advertising and related efforts used on behalf of a shopping center in the attainment of predetermined goals.

Center Rate: reduced advertising rate arranged between center and publication for use by tenants during cooperative centerwide advertised events.

Circular/Shopper: a preprinted special section with a cover page followed by ads relating to a specific center and event. Hand delivered or inserted into an area publication.

Circulation: the number of copies of a newspaper or circular sold and distributed.

Column Depth and Width: measure of print material in inches, lines, or picas.

Column Inch: print advertising term; one column wide by one inch deep.

Combination Rate: a common rate charged for insertion in two or more publications.

Commercial: an advertising message delivered on radio or television.

Common Area: the walkways and areas onto which the stores in a center face, which conduct the flow of customer traffic.

Community acceptance: the recognition of a shopping center by its market area as an integral part of the community, as well as a purveyor of goods and services.

Continuity: an advertising message that runs consistently; used for image building.

Contract: media term. A written agreement (usually 1 year duration) to use a specified amount of space (print) or air time (radio and TV).

Cooperative Pages: single or facing pages divided into equal sized box ads, headed with a banner giving event details. All ads in same type face; no logos permitted.

Cooperative Section: see *circular/shopper*; mailer.

Copy and Layout: print media term; the visual and copy components of an ad to be typeset by a publication. Usually requires a proof.

Copy and Layout Deadline: the lead time required to produce an ad and furnish a proof prior to publication.

Cover Page: lead page of a cooperative special section that promotes the theme, event day, center hours, and other pertinent information.

Deadline: the final date advertising material can reach a publication prior to printing.

Demographics: vital statistics of the marketing area; that is, average income, age, number of children, cost of homes, education, and ethnic factors.

Distribution: area covered by the circulation of a publication.

Door Busters: small groups of sharply reduced merchandise, with incomplete assortments.

Double Truck: print media term; the two centerfold facing pages of ads, including gutter space.

Drive Time: a radio term, referring to automobile commuting time; usually 7 A.M. to 9 A.M. and 4:30 P.M. to 6:30 P.M..

Finished Mechanical: completed paste-up of an ad in which visual and copy components are ready for reproduction by the print medium.

Format: the pattern of an advertisement or publication; typeface, size, shape.

Frequency: refers to consistency of advertising; frequent advertising usually results in a rate reduction.

Glossies: reproducible prints of ads, supplied to publications.

Graphics: descriptive techniques including sketches, photographs, and all other visual components of an ad.

Gutter Space: blank space inside of newspaper pages.

Headline: the heading of a printed advertisement.

Horizontal: term applies to shopping center as an entity; that is, as one horizontal department store.

Image Building: a consistent program of advertising and publicity, designed to favorably portray a shopping center to the market area in terms of community involvement and the availability of goods and services.

In-House Agency: installed by owner-developers with a group of shopping centers to create a desired image through the use of the various media; also to provide guidance to the various centers for their budget and promotion programs.

Insert: a preprinted section, delivered by insertion in the publication.

Insertion Order: written instructions to the publication authorizing insertion of an advertisement, and providing specifications.

Institutional Advertising: used to build the reputation of a center as the most desirable complex in the area offering goods and services to the consumer.

Kiosks: booths located in the common areas of the center-mall and generally housing small-item merchandise or services; for example: hosiery, photo developing.

Layout: sketch and design of an ad.

Letterpress: the process of printing direct from an inked, raised surface upon which the paper is impressed.

Local Rate: the rate offered to advertisers who do not benefit from coverage beyond their own market area; substantially below national rates.

Logo: stylized characteristic symbol for sustained identification of a corporation, product, or service.

Low-End: merchandise that has been sharply reduced from original prices, used for sidewalk, moonlight, midnight, and similar limited period sale events.

Mailer: preprinted special section with a cover page followed by ads relating to a specific center and event, and delivered by mail.

Mall Manager: supervises operation and maintenance of center common areas and parking lot, manages personnel, and acts in liaison with owner/developer and individual tenants.

Markdown: reduction in retail price of merchandise, primarily for clearance, special sales events, or to meet competition.

Market Area: surrounding communities from which the center draws shoppers.

Marketing Director: responsible for all promotion director activities as well as: continuing market research for dissemination to tenants and enforcing lease agreements relating to promotion violations.

Market Research: a survey conducted for the developer before commitment to build and, in some instances, on a recurring basis. Reports define demographics and psychographics of the market area.

Mat: material from which an advertisement is printed.

Media Representative: liaison for center merchants in cooperative promotions; associated with a publication or an electronic medium.

Merchants Association: the tenant group organized to promote the center through cooperative advertising, public relations activity and community involvement.

Merchants Association Dues: the financial obligation of member tenants and landlord, fixed by a predetermined structure, and used for centerwide promotion and community activities.

Midnight Sale: centerwide, merchant-association sponsored, low-end, off-price promotion, generally continuing until 11 P.M. or midnight; one night only.

Mix: a combination of the media, or tenants, or merchandise, etc., that provides choices for the consumer, and balance to the shopping center.

Moonlite Sale: see *midnight sale.* Hours usually not later than 11 P.M..

National Rate: the rate offered to national advertisers (many markets). Used by both the print and electronic media, and substantially more costly than a local rate.

Off-Price Advertising: promotes price reduced merchandise during a specific sale period.

Offset Printing: process in which an inked impression from a plate is made on a rubber-blanketed cylinder and then transferred to the paper being printed.

Open Rate: print media term; the line or inch cost paid by advertisers without contracts or center rate availability.

Open Windows: display areas, fronting the mall, with no glass enclosure or barriers; used in enclosed malls only; exposes store interior to mall passers-by.

Participation: tenants joining in a common promotion effort sponsored by the center.

Picas: print media measurement term; one-sixth of an inch, or 6 picas to an inch.

Plot Plan: blueprint of a center showing location and square footage of all tenants, as well as surface facilities.

Pre-empt: an electronic media term, for time sold at a lower rate, and subject to resale by the station if a higher rate is offered.

Preferred Positioning: a print media term, referring to desirable positioning of an ad; that is, right-hand pages 3 or 5, or preceding centerfold.

Primary Market: geographic term used to define the immediate trading area of a shopping center.

Prime Time: a television term, denoting the hours TV viewing is at its peak; usually 7:30 P.M. to 11 P.M., local time.

Promotion Director: supervises advertising, exhibits, special activities or events, press, and public relations as they apply to the center as an entity.

Proof: printed copy of publication-set ad; submitted to advertiser for corrections and/or approval prior to publication.

Psychographics: the motivating forces that influence shopping patterns and consumer behavior.

Public Relations: the establishment and maintenance of good will, promulgated by participation and concern for communitywide activities.

Publicity Release: information with news value distributed to the media for purposes of favorably influencing consumers.

Pub-Set: ad prepared by a publication when submitted as copy and layout.

Radio: AAA Time: Monday through Friday—6:00 A.M. to 9:00 A.M. and Monday through Friday—4:30 P.M. to 6:30 P.M.

Radio: AA Time: Monday through Friday—9:00 A.M. to 4:30 P.M.

Radio: A Time: Monday through Friday—6:30 P.M. to sign off and Saturday and Sunday—all day.

Rate Card: a published list of advertising rates and other related data obtained from individual publications.

Rates and Data Book: a publication that lists all pertinent information relating to newspapers published in the United States.

Representative or Rep: the salesperson or contact for any medium.

Run-of-Paper: the placement of a newspaper advertisement in any portion as determined by the publication. Referred to as R.O.P.

Run of Station: pre-emptible spot commercials bought for airing within a station's schedule, timed at their discretion.

Secondary Market: geographic term used to designate areas outside the primary market; the fringes of the market and beyond.

Short-Rate: print media term which means that the paper charges at higher rate if advertiser does not fulfill contract.

Sig-Cut: see logo.

Sidewalk Sale: a centerwide, merchant association sponsored, off-price, low-end promotion; merchandise is displayed from common areas fronting each store.

Space Deadline: the lead time required by publication to reserve advertising space for a specific date.

Special Event: a centerwide, merchant association sponsored promotion aimed at generating increased customer traffic.

Tear Sheet: printed, dated copy of ad as it appeared; generally submitted with invoice as proof of publication.

Teaser Ads: small ads, run in advance of a major effort, to arouse interest in a forthcoming campaign.

Traffic-Building Device: a center-sponsored promotional activity designed to stimulate customer traffic.

Unanimity: singleness of purpose; exemplified by promotion of a shopping center as a total entity.

Vertical: term used to relate a shopping center to a department store in urban areas.

White Spaces: print media term referring to the blank space in an ad.

APPENDIX A

Invitation to First Merchants Association Meeting

TO: ALL TENANTS, PRINCIPALS AND MANAGEMENT

Our first and very important Merchants Association Meeting will be held on Thursday, June 14th. We will meet initially in the Center Court (Lower Level) for an on-sight inspection of Bel Air Shopping City at 4:00 P.M.

Refreshments will be served after the tour and we will depart by 5:30 P.M. for the Red Lion Inn, with cocktails and dinner in the Cedar Room starting at 6:00 P.M. For your driving convenience, a directional map showing the exact locations of Bel Air Shopping City (U.S. 95 at Exit 9) and the Red Lion Inn (intersection of Routes 280 and 95) is enclosed herewith. These social functions will be followed by the Merchants Association Meeting, starting promptly at 8:00 P.M.

The major purpose of this meeting is to present the Articles of Incorporation, approve the Bylaws, elect a Board of Directors (and their officers), and to present and have approved the Budget for the Grand Opening and first Fiscal Year.

For your advance information, attached is the Agenda outlining the subjects to be resolved at the meeting. If this Merchants Association is to become an effective organization working for our best interests, it is essential that every tenant be represented, and that he or she have the authority to vote on the topics listed in the Agenda.

We have enclosed a form on which you will please indicate your representative(s) who will attend. Please complete the information requested and return the form to:

Mr. George Hixson
Bel Air Shopping City
3110 Ramsey Avenue
Asheville, N.C. 28801

We are looking forward to meeting you and your fellow Bel Air merchants.

Sincerely yours,

George Hixson

George Hixson

Note: If the Promotion Fund Concept is used, hold the meeting and adapt this letter to the situation. Pre-opening and annual meetings with tenants are important for both Promotion Funds and Merchant Associations.

Response Card

BEL AIR MERCHANTS ASSOCIATION MEETING

June 14, 19XX

RED LION INN, ASHEVILLE, NORTH CAROLINA

A maximum of two representatives may attend this opening dinner meeting as guests of the landlord-developer. One (1) additional guest may attend at a cost of $12.00 payable with your R.S.V.P.

REPRESENTATIVE(S) TO ATTEND:

_____	_____	_____
STORE NAME	STORE NAME	STORE NAME
_____	_____	_____
REPRESENTATIVE'S NAME	REPRESENTATIVE'S NAME	REPRESENTATIVE'S NAME
_____	_____	_____
REPRESENTATIVE'S POSITION	REPRESENTATIVE'S POSITION	REPRESENTATIVE'S POSITION
_____	_____	_____
TELEPHONE NUMBER	TELEPHONE NUMBER	TELEPHONE NUMBER

R.S.V.P. BY

MAY 15, 19XX

Agenda

Opening Remarks

Franklin Forsythe, Sr.
Executive Vice President
Franklin Development Corp.

Construction Progress on the Mall

William Steiger
Vice President/Construction
Franklin Development Corp.

Election of Board of Directors

Membership

Presentation of Board of Directors

Frank Lampert
United Shoes
Chairman of Nominating
Committee

Discussion & Vote on Articles of Incorporation and Bylaws

George Hixson
Promotion Director

Presentation of Preopening, Opening, and First 30-Day
Budget and Advertising Program

Ace Advertising, Inc.

Approval of Opening Budget and Advertising Program
(Above)

George Hixson

Responsibility List for
First Merchants Association Meeting

Bel Air Shopping City Merchants Association Reception and Organizational Meeting

Date: Thursday, June 14, 19XX

Times & Places:

4:00 P.M.—Inspection, libation, and refreshments—
Center Court, Lower Level

6:00 P.M.—Reception, cocktail hour, and dinner,
Red Lion Inn, Routes 280 & 95, Asheville, N.C.

8:00 P.M.—Merchants Association Meeting, Red Lion Inn,
Asheville, N.C.

Name(s)	
	Invitations
George Hixson and Franklin Forsythe, Sr.	**1.** Mailing list to be prepared, including all tenant Home, District, and Local office contacts who will be responsible for decisions and have authority to vote on motions.
Franklin Forsythe, Sr.	**2.** Letter of invitation to go to the above by May 3, 19XX. To include Reservation Form and location map. R.S.V.P. George Hixson.
George Hixson	**3.** Hixson to build attendance list from R.S.V.P. Use for head count and name tags. Also advise Forsythe about designees who can guarantee a quorum.
Franklin Forsythe, Sr.	**4.** Mail final Bylaws to all principal representatives for tenants by May 15, 19XX.
	Preplanning
George Hixson and Earl Gordon	**1.** Negotiations with Red Lion Inn to be closed by May 17, 19XX for use of their Cedar Room. Cocktail Hour, Dinner menu, and price per person for the facilities and services to be completed.
George Hixson and Earl Gordon	**2.** Cedar Room to be floor planned to show placement of all furniture, fixtures, equipment, and personnel by May 24, 19XX.
George Hixson	**3.** Hand out materials to be edited, produced, and ready by June 1, 19XX.
George Hixson	**4.** Temporary store fronts to be completed by June 7, 19XX.
Earl Gordon	**5.** Mall common area cleaning and security schedules set by May 24, 19XX.
George Hixson	**6.** Tenant signs on all unidentified store fronts. Use mall and tenant logos. Completed by June 11, 19XX.
	Physical Set-Up (Mall Inspection)
George Hixson and Earl Gordon	**1.** Directional signs to mall entrance (Southeast Lower Level) to be in place by June 11, 19XX. In-mall signs in place Noon, June 12, 1979.
Earl Gordon	**2.** Trained traffic, parking, and in-mall security on Bel Air site by 3:00 P.M. June 14th. All officers will have red coned flashlights. Four officers for traffic; two in Mall during inspection.

Earl Gordon	**3.** Common areas and parking lot cleaned. Schedule is June 11, 12, and 13 with touch-up all day the 14th. Two porters on duty from 3:00 to 6:00 P.M. in Center Court to police area during inspection.
George Hixson and Earl Gordon	**4.** Directional signs to Red Lion Inn mounted on security vehicles at Route 95 (Raleigh Road)—Exit 9.
George Hixson	**5.** Equipment and personnel:

a. Reception table with floral piece, guestbook, pens, hand out Auto ID tags to drivers for Red Lion Inn parking, table cover (to floor), 2 chairs, ID sign, Tenant Directories.

b. Three bars with all set-ups (mixes, ice, cups, supplies).

c. Buy liquor for 150—Set-ups from caterer.

d. Set eight tables with covers with six chairs per table.

e. Set one large center table with cover for snacks and floral piece.

f. Two Hostesses; three bartenders, four waitresses, and all Bel Air Shopping City representatives.

g. Adequate trash receptacles; ash trays, matches, napkins, plastic plates, forks & knives, 2-gallon coffee urn and cups.

Physical Set-up (Dinner Meeting—Red Lion Inn)

George Hixson	**1.** Exterior directional signs at parking entrance and easeled signs to Cedar Room in lobby.
George Hixson	**2.** Security officers with Red coned flashlights to assist parking in designated areas for vehicles showing ID tag.
George Hixson	**3.** Tables in lobby for hand out of Merchant Kits with name tags attached. Have back-up kits and tags for added guests and list them for billing purposes. Two Hostesses.
George Hixson	**4.** Follow floor plan for table placement, audio-visual equipment (all previously checked out and backed-up).
George Hixson	**5.** Cocktail area will have two bars with full set-ups. Light snacks on large table in central area.

George Hixson	**6.** Dinner to begin promptly at 7:00 P.M. with 12 waitresses to serve.
George Hixson	**7.** Head table to be elevated dais with seating arrangements identified by name cards.
George Hixson	**8.** Public address system to work off house system using five microphones; one at head table, others interspersed at guest tables. Two tape recorders—one to tape program, one for the jingle. One operator for both.
George Hixson	**9.** Small combo to play background music for cocktail party.
	10. Qualified photographer to be on hand at 5:30 P.M.

Agenda—Red Lion Inn

Franklin Forsythe, Sr.	**1.** Chairman calls meeting to order. Opening remarks.
Franklin Forsythe, Sr.	**2.** Introduction of Dais.
Franklin Forsythe, Sr.	**3.** *Articles of Incorporation and Bylaws—Discussion, Motion, Second and Approval.
George Hixson	**4.** *Election and presentation of Board of Directors.
George Hixson	**5.** Presentation of Grand Opening and First Fiscal-Year Budget. Marketing Information.
Fred Perry	**6.** ACE Advertising, Inc., presentation of Grand Opening and First Fiscal-Year Promotions. Audio-visual and discussion.
Franklin Forsythe, Sr.	**7.** Discussion, Motion, Second and Approval of Budgets and Programs.
Franklin Forsythe, Sr.	**8.** General discussion of items relating to Grand Opening. Question and Answer—twenty minutes maximum.
Franklin Forsythe Sr.	**9.** Motion and Second for adjournment by 10:00 P.M.
Franklin Forsythe, Sr.	**10.** *Board of Directors hold short meeting after adjournment to name officers.
George Hixson	**11.** Have steno to take minutes of business action.
George Hixson	**12.** *Have hand signature cards ready for authorized signatures of officers.

*Substitute discussion of promotion fund, if no merchants association.

Rehearsal

Franklin Forsythe, Sr.
George Hixson
Earl Gordon
Fred Perry

8:00 P.M. Wednesday, June 13, 19XX—Red Lion Inn.

Set-up Presentation—Red Lion Inn

George Hixson and
Fred Perry

1. ACE will have projectors and screen set, and adjusted. They will also have all art renderings distributed about the room on easels.

George Hixson and
Fred Perry

2. Merchant Kits to include:

Left Pocket —*Articles of Incorporation
          — Tenant Directory
          —*Bylaws
          — Agenda
          — Attendee List

Right Pocket—Media Package from ACE
          —Trade area map
          —Print coverage map
          —Opening Assessment & Budget
          —First-Year Assessment
           & Budget
          —Letter of Welcome to
           specific tenants and
           their opening assessment
           dues.

*Substitute promotion fund information if no merchants association.

Outline of Grand Opening Countdown

1. *May 17, 19XX (Thursday)—*
Advertising Meeting with Department Stores

2. *July 9, 19XX (Monday)—*
Merchants Association Promotion Meeting

3. *August 7, 19XX (Tuesday)—*
V.I.P. Civic Mall Reception

4. *August 9, 19XX (Thursday)—*
Media Reception

5. *October 3, 19XX (Wednesday)—*
Preopening Reception

6. *October 4, 19XX (Thursday)—*
Grand Opening

7. *November 3, 19XX (Saturday)—*
End of 30-Day Grand Opening Period

APPENDIX B

Articles of Incorporation for Merchants Association

ARTICLE I

We, the undersigned, Joseph Roberts, Donald Long, and Robert Hawkins, being natural-born persons aged 21 years or more and citizens of the United States, do hereby associate ourselves as incorporators with the intention of forming a corporation under, and by virtue of, the General Laws of the State of North Carolina.

ARTICLE II

The name of the corporation (hereinafter to be called the Corporation) is BEL AIR SHOPPING CITY MERCHANTS ASSOCIATION, INC.

ARTICLE III

The purpose for which the Corporation is organized are as follows:

(1) To develop and improve in all lawful and proper ways the business interests of all merchants in the Bel Air Shopping City, Asheville, North Carolina (hereinafter called Bel Air), and in the furtherance of such purpose to foster uniformity in all promotional programs and publicity, cooperative advertising, special events, decoration, store hours, and all other endeavors for the common benefit of all the merchants in said Shopping City.

(2) To accept, receive, take hold by bequest, acquire, purchase, exchange, lease, transfer, grant or otherwise, any property of any kind, real or personal.

(3) To sell, convey, mortgage, transfer, lease, exchange or otherwise dispose of any such property, real or personal, as required for the purposes of the Corporation.

(4) To incur debts, negotiate contracts, borrow money, issue bonds, notes and other obligations; to secure them by mortgage or deed of trust of all or any part of the property and income of the Corporation.

(5) To execute all or any part of the foregoing objects as principal, factor, agent, contractor, or otherwise, either alone or in conjunction with any person, firm, association, or corporation, and, in conducting its business and for the purpose of attaining or furthering any or all of its objectives, to enter into and implement any contracts, and to exercise any powers proper or convenient for the accomplishment of any of the objectives and purposes enumerated herein or incidental to the powers specified, or which at any time may appear conducive to or expedient for the accomplishment of any of such objects and purposes.

The foregoing purpose shall, except when otherwise expressed, be in no way limited or restricted by reference to, or inference from, the terms of any other clause of this or any other article of the charter or the Corporation, and shall each be regarded as independent, and interpreted as powers as well as purposes of the Corporation.

The Corporation shall be authorized to exercise and enjoy all the powers, rights, and privileges granted to, or conferred upon, corporations of a similar character by the General Laws of the State of North Carolina now or hereafter in force, and the enumeration of the foregoing purpose shall not be deemed to exclude any powers, rights, or privileges so granted or conferred.

ARTICLE IV

The post office address of the principal office of the Corporation in this State is c/o Bel Air Shopping City, 3110 W. Ramsey Avenue, Asheville, North Carolina 28801. The name and post office address of the initial resident agent of the Corporation is George Hixson, Suite 32, at 3110 W. Ramsey Avenue, Asheville, North Carolina 28801

ARTICLE V

The Corporation is not authorized to issue capital stock. The membership of the Corporation shall be comprised of (i) occupants of retail or service space in the Shopping City Area incorporated as Bel Air Shopping City, in the City of Asheville, Fayette County, North Carolina, (ii) other occupants of space in the Shopping City Area required by lease or other agreement with their landlords to become members of the Corporation, and (iii) Bel Air Shopping City, Inc., owner of said Shopping Center Area, and its successor or successors in ownership to all or any part of said Shopping Center Area. Members shall be entitled to vote as prescribed by the Bylaws.

ARTICLE VI

The number of directors of this Corporation shall be eleven (11), which number may be increased pursuant to the Bylaws of the Corporation, but shall never be less than eleven (11). However, until the directors are duly chosen and qualify, George Hixson, Franklyn Forsythe, Sr., William Steiger, and Donald Reese shall be designated as members of the steering committee and serve as advisors to Bel Air Shopping City management.

ARTICLE VII

The following provisions are hereby adopted for the purpose of defining, limiting, and regulating the powers of the Corporation and of the directors and members:

(1) The Corporation shall be operated as a nonprofit corporation and no part of its net earnings (if any) shall inure to the benefit of any member, officer, or director of the Corporation. In the event of the dissolution of the Corporation, all accrued net earnings, if any, and all net assets, if any, shall be distributed among members in good standing at the time of such dissolution in proportion to the amount of dues and other assessments paid by such members during the last full fiscal year prior to the dissolution; or, as an alternative, all net assets shall not be distributed to members, but turned over to a charitable or educational organization with the final determination made by the Board of Directors.

(2) The Board of Directors shall have power to determine at any time whether and to what extent and at what time and places and under what conditions and regulations the books, accounts, and documents of the Corporation shall be open to the inspection of members, except as otherwise provided by statute or by the Bylaws; and, except as so provided, no member shall have any right to inspect any book, account, or document of the Corporation unless authorized so to do by resolution of the Board of Directors.

(3) Any director, individually, or any firm of which any director may be a member, or any corporation or association of which any director may be an officer or director, or in which any director may be interested financially or otherwise, may be a party to, or may be pecuniarily or otherwise interested in, any contract or transaction of the Corporation, and in the absence of fraud, no contract or other transaction shall be thereby affected or invalidated; provided that in case a director, or a firm of which a director is a member, is so interested, such fact shall be disclosed or shall have been known to the Board of Directors or a majority thereof. However, no director of the Corporation who is also a director or officer of or interested in such other corporation or association, or who, or the firm of which he is a member, is so interested, may be counted in determining the existence of a quorum at any meeting of the Board of Directors of the Corporation which shall authorize any such contract or transaction, and may not vote thereat to authorize any such contract or transaction.

(4) Any contract, transaction, or act of the Corporation or of the directors which shall be ratified by a majority of the votes cast by the members of any annual meeting at which a quorum is present and voting, or at any special meeting of which a quorum is present and voting, called for such purpose, shall so far as permitted by law be as valid and as binding as though ratified by every member of the Corporation.

(5) Unless the Bylaws otherwise provide, any officer or employee of the Corporation (other than a director) may be removed at any time with or without cause by the Board of Directors or by any committee or superior officer upon whom such power of removal may be conferred by the Bylaws or by authority of the Board of Directors.

ARTICLE VIII
The period of duration of the Corporation shall be perpetual.

IN WITNESS WHEREOF, we have signed these Articles of Incorporation on _____, 19XX.

_____

Joseph Roberts

_____

Donald Long

_____

Robert Hawkins

Witnessed By:

_____

William J. Rose

STATE OF NORTH CAROLINA, COUNTY OF FAYETTE, to wit

I HEREBY CERTIFY that on _____, 19xx, before me, a Notary Public of the State of North Carolina, in and for Fayette County, personally appeared Joseph Roberts, Donald Long, and Robert Hawkins, and severally acknowledged the foregoing Articles of Incorporation to be their act.

WITNESS my hand and Notarial Seal the day and year last above written.

_____

William J. Rose, Notary Public
My Commission Expires: July 1, 19xx.

94

Merchants Association Bylaws I

Article I

SECTION 1—Membership. There shall be two classes of membership in this Association: Active Members and Associate Members.

(i) Only a Corporation, Partnership, or an Individual with businesses or professions located at, and operating in Bel Air Shopping City shall be eligible to be Active Members. All such Corporations, Partnerships, or Individuals shall be active members from the time the Merchants Association is incorporated, as provided for by lease between the afore named Corporations, Partnerships, and Individuals and Bel Air Shopping City, Inc. The owner of the real property, known as Bel Air Shopping City, Inc., hereinafter referred to as "Landlord," shall also be an Active Member from the date of Incorporation of the Merchants Association with the rights, privileges, and obligations set forth hereinafter.

(ii) Any other Corporation, Partnership, or Individual making application to be an Associate Member in this Corporation, and who or which in the opinion of the majority of the Board of Trustees has a common interest in the objectives and goals of this Corporation as set forth in the Certificates of Incorporation shall be engaged in a legitimate business or profession and shall otherwise be worthy of membership, may be elected an Associate Member if such application shall be approved by a majority of the Board of Trustees. Associate Members shall be entitled only to such notices, if any, of meetings or other activities, as these Bylaws shall prescribe that such Members shall receive, and shall at no time have any right to vote at any meeting of this Corporation.

SECTION 2—Annual Meeting. All annual meetings of the members of the Merchants Assocation shall be held in the Community Room of Bel Air Shopping City in Fayette County, State of North Carolina, on the first Wednesday in October of each year (or such date and/or place within Fayette County as may be designated by the Board of Trustees) for the annual election of Trustees, for the transaction of all business requiring approval of the General Membership, and other such general business as may be brought before the Membership. If the first Wednesday in October shall be a legal holiday, the annual meeting of the members shall be held on the next Wednesday following which is not a legal holiday, and at the same hour and place. Such annual meetings shall be general meetings, that is to say, open for the transaction of any business within the powers of the Corporation without special notice of specific business, except in any case in which special notice is required by the Charter or by these Bylaws.

SECTION 3—Special General Membership Meetings. Special meetings of the members of the Association may be called at any time, by a majority of the Board of Trustees, either by actual vote or by written agreement.

(i) Upon receipt of this special meeting request, delivered in writing to the President, Secretary, or any Trustee, of a majority of all the Active Members, it shall be the duty of the President to call forthwith a meeting of the Association members.

(ii) If the person to whom such request in writing shall have been delivered, shall fail to issue a call for such meeting within three days after the receipt of such request, then Active Members, constituting a majority of all the Active Members, may do so by activating the notice set forth in Section 4 of this Article I.

SECTION 4 -Notice of Meetings. Written or printed notice of every annual or special meeting of members (except of any meeting called by the members as provided in Section 3 of this Article I) must state the place, day, and hour of such meeting and shall be given at least ten days prior thereto to each member.

(i) Such notice shall be personally delivered at the residence or usual place of business, or by mailing it, postage prepaid, and addressed to each member as the address on the records of the Corporation. Notice of every special meeting shall state also the business to be transacted thereat, and no business shall be transacted at such special meeting except that specifically named in the notice.

(ii) Notice of special meetings called by the Active Members, as provided in Section 3 of this Article I, shall be given by written communication to reach 10 days prior to such meeting and directed to each Active Member at the address that appears on the books of this Corporation. It shall not be requisite to the validity of any special meeting of the members that notice thereof, whether prescribed by statute, by the Charter or these Bylaws, shall have been given to any member who attends in person or by proxy, or who, if absent, waives notice thereof in writing filed with the records of the meeting either before or after the holding thereof. No notice of an adjourned meeting of members need be given. Notice of any general membership meeting need be given only to the Active Members.

SECTION 5 —Quorum. At any meeting of the members a quorum necessary to conduct the business thereof shall be seventeen Active Members.

(i) In the absence of a quorum, the members present in person or by proxy at any meeting (or adjournment thereof) may by vote of a majority of the Active Members so present adjourn the meeting from time to time, but not for a period of over ten days at any one time without notice other than by an announcement at the meeting, until a quorum shall attend.

(ii) At any such adjourned meeting at which a quorum shall be present, any business may be transacted which might have been transacted at the meeting as originally notified.

SECTION 6—Voting. At any meeting of the members, only Active Members shall be entitled to vote.

(i) Each Active Member shall be entitled to cast one vote, and the Landlord shall be entitled to cast one vote.

(ii) Any action taken shall be effective and valid if authorized by at least a majority of all the votes to which all the members present in person or by proxy at a duly constituted meeting shall be entitled, provided Landlord be present in person or by proxy and has cast his vote.

SECTION 7–Resignation and Removal. Active and Associate Members:

(i) Active Members are obligated by lease arrangement to continue Merchant Association membership while tenants in Bel Air Shopping City and to follow these Bylaws in their activities relevant to the Merchants Association.

(ii) Associate Members may resign at any time by submitting their resignation to the Board of Trustees. This action does not relieve said member of any indebtedness to the Association. He may be removed from his Associate Membership by the affirmative vote of at least three-fourths (3/4) of the Board of Trustees of the Association, with or without cause, and such action shall be binding upon such Associate Members.

Article II

Board of Trustees

SECTION 1—Election. The affairs and activities of the Corporation, except as otherwise provided by statute, by the Charter or by these Bylaws, shall be conducted and managed by its Board of Trustees, the members of which shall be determined at each annual meeting of the members of the Corporation, and shall be not less than eleven, nor more than seventeen, with representatives of the Landlord, Heely's, Smith-Gordon, Erlinger Co., and Wasserman's holding permanent assignments as Trustees. The remaining members of the Board of Trustees shall be Active Members elected by the Active Members of the Corporation at their annual meeting, and each Trustee so elected shall hold office until the annual meeting held next after his election and until his successor shall have been duly chosen and qualified or until he is unable to serve for personal reasons, resigns, or shall have been removed. The permanent Trustees shall serve at the pleasure of the landlord and can be removed from office only by him. The Board of Trustees shall keep minutes of its meetings and a full account of its transactions.

SECTION 2—Regular Meetings. Regular meetings of the Board of Trustees shall be held as soon as practicable after every annual meeting of the members of the Corporation, and thereafter on such dates as may be fixed from time to time by resolution of the Board.

SECTION 3—Special Meetings. Special meetings of the Board of Trustees shall be held whenever called by the President or by a majority of the Board, either in writing or by vote.

SECTION 4—Place of Meetings. Regular and special meetings of the Board shall be held at the principal office of the Corporation in Bel Air Shopping City. However, the Board of Trustees may schedule regular and special meetings, at such other place or places as it may from time to time determine, but the meeting places must be within Fayette County, North Carolina.

SECTION 5—Notice of Meetings. Notice of the place, day and hour of every regular and special meeting shall be given to each Trustee at least three days before the meeting by delivering the same to him personally or by sending the same to him by telegram, or by depositing the same at his residence or usual place of business, or by mailing such notice, postage prepaid, at least four days prior to the meeting, addressed to him at his last recorded post office address, as shown by the records of the Association. It shall not be requisite to the validity of any meeting of the Board of Trustees that notice thereof shall have been given to any Trustee who attends such meetings, or who, if absent, waives notice thereof in writing filed with the records of the meeting either before or after the holding thereof. Twenty-four hours' notice of any adjourned meeting of the Board must be given the Trustees.

SECTION 6—Quorum. A majority of the number of Trustees in office shall constitute a quorum for the transaction of business at any meeting of the Board of Trustees; but if at any meeting there be less than a quorum present, a majority of those present may adjourn the meeting from time to time, but not for a period of over ten days at any one time. Seventy-two hours' notice shall be given the Trustee of the time and place to which the meeting has been adjourned, which procedure shall be followed until a quorum shall be present. At any such adjourned meeting at which a quorum shall be present, any business may be transacted which might have been transacted at the meeting as originally notified.

SECTION 7—Vacancies. Vacancies in the Board of Trustees (other than in Trustees appointed by Landlord) shall be filled only by Active Members of the Corporation who shall elect new Trustees to hold office for the unexpired terms of the Trustees whose place shall be vacant and until his successor shall be duly chosen and qualified. Vacancies among the Trustees serving at the pleasure of the Landlord shall be filled by his appointment. Trustees elected to fill vacancies caused by an increase in the number of Trustees shall hold office until the next succeeding annual meeting of members of the Corporation and until their successors are duly elected and qualified.

Article III

Officers

SECTION 1—Executive Officers. The executive officers of the Corporation shall be a President, one Vice-President, a Secretary, and a Treasurer. The President and Vice-President shall be selected from among the membership of the Board of Trustees. The remaining officers need not be Trustees, but must be Active Members. Officers shall be elected by the Trustees at their first regular meeting after the annual meeting of members, and each shall hold office until the regular meeting of Trustees following the next annual meeting of members and until his successor is duly elected and qualified or until his demise, resignation, or removal. Two or more offices (except those of President and Vice-President) may be held by the same person. The Trustees shall have the power at any regular or special meeting to remove any officer, with or without cause, and such action shall be binding on the officer so removed.

SECTION 2—President. The President shall be the chief officer of the Corporation. He shall, when present, preside at all meetings of the General Membership and Trustees; he shall have general management and direction of the affairs of the Association and all powers ordinarily exercised by the President of a Corporation; he shall have authority to sign and execute, in the name of the Association, all authorized contracts and other instruments; he shall annually prepare a full statement of the affairs of the Corporation which shall be submitted at the annual meeting of the members.

SECTION 3—Vice-President. In the absence or disability of the President, the Vice-President selected for this purpose by the Board of Trustees shall perform all the duties of the President, and when so acting, shall have such additional powers and duties as may from time to time be assigned to him by the Board of Trustees.

SECTION 4—Secretary. The Secretary shall keep the minutes of the meetings of members and the Board of Trustees in books provided for that purpose; he shall see that all notices are duly given in accordance with the provisions of the Charter, Bylaws, and as required by law; he shall be the custodian of the records and of the Corporate Seal of the Corporation; he shall see that the Corporate Seal is affixed to all documents the execution of which on behalf of the Corporation under its seal is duly authorized, and when so affixed may attest the same; and, in general, he shall perform all duties ordinarily incident to the office of a Secretary of a Corporation, and such other duties as, from time to time, may be assigned to him by the Board of Trustees or by the President. In the absence of the Secretary, the Treasurer will act for the Secretary.

SECTION 5—Treasurer. The Treasurer shall have charge and be responsible for all funds, securities, receipts, and disbursements of the Corporation and shall deposit or cause to be deposited in the name of the Corporation all money or other valuables in such banks or other depositories as shall from time to time be selected by the Board of Trustees; he shall render to the President and to the Board whenever requested an account of the financial condition of the Corporation; and, in general, he shall perform all the duties ordinarily incident to the office of Treasurer of a Corporation and such other duties as may be assigned to him by the Board of Trustees or by the President. In the absence of the Treasurer, the Secretary shall act for the Treasurer.

SECTION 6—Vacancies. A vacancy occurring in any office shall be filled by vote of the Board of Trustees for the unexpired portion of the term.

SECTION 7—Supplementary Officers. In addition to the executive officers, there may be appointed by the Board of Trustees at their discretion, an Assistant Secretary and an Assistant Treasurer who shall have such duties as the Board of Trustees shall prescribe.

SECTION 8—Promotion, Advertising, and Public Relations. The Landlord shall have the right, at his option and discretion, to appoint the Promotion, Advertising, and Public Relations personnel for the Association, but shall seek the advice of the Board of Trustees prior to making commitment. The fees of such personnel must be competitive with those charged by others conducting business in the area. The Landlord may, at his option, but with prior consultation with the Board of Trustees, terminate the services of such personnel or agency. The Landlord may also appoint a Secretary to the Association without prior consultation or approval and shall have the right of dismissal, with or without cause, and without prior consultation of the Board of Trustees.

SECTION 9—Compensation of Promotion, Advertising, and Public Relations Personnel. The Landlord may, at his option, add such personnel to his payroll, but all payments made be deducted in their entirety from his contribution to the Merchants Association.

Article IV

Merchants Association Dues

SECTION 1—Assessments. There shall be assessments against Association Members for the promotion of Bel Air Shopping City, in the amounts incorporated into leases of all tenants, and Landlord shall contribute one-quarter (¼) of the aggregate amount paid by said tenants.

SECTION 2—Dues Increases. The Board of Trustees may, by majority vote, call for a general membership meeting to request an increase in the dues structure, requiring approval by majority vote of Active Members.

Landlord will similarly increase his contribution by paying one-quarter of the additional dues voted.

SECTION 3—Bills and Payment. Dues shall be billed quarterly by the Association Secretary, and are payable ten (10) days after receipt of such invoice.

SECTION 4—Delinquency. Non-payment of dues within thirty (30) days after receipt of the invoice will result in suspension of all rights and privileges set forth in the Charter and Bylaws of the Association. Reinstatement will occur ten (10) days after payment of such delinquent dues.

Article V

Sundry Provisions

SECTION 1—Seal. The Seal of the Corporation shall be square in form with the name of the Corporation and the words "State of North Carolina" inscribed in the center surrounded by the words "Incorporated 19xx."

SECTION 2—Checks, Money Orders, Drafts, etc. All checks, drafts or money orders, notes, and other evidences of indebtedness issued in the name of this Corporation shall be signed and/or countersigned by such persons who from time to time shall be designated by resolution of the Board of Trustees.

SECTION 3—Bonds. The Board of Trustees may require any officers, agent, or employee of the Corporation to give a bond to the Corporation for the faithful discharge of his duties, in such amount, on such conditions, and with such sureties as may be required by the Board.

SECTION 4—Amendments. These Bylaws, or any of them, or any additional or supplementary Bylaws may be altered or repealed and new Bylaws may be adopted by the Active Members at any annual meeting of said Members without notice, or at any special meeting of said Members, the notice of which shall detail the terms of the proposed amendment. The Board of Trustees at any time may make, alter, and repeal additional and supplementary Bylaws not inconsistent with these Bylaws and any Bylaws adopted by the members of the Corporation; but any such additional or supplementary Bylaws may be altered or repealed only by the Active Members of the Corporation as provided in this Section. No amendment of these Bylaws, or additions thereto, may, however, alter or affect the provisions of these Bylaws relating to Landlord, and the rights and privileges granted it.

Merchants Association Bylaws II

Article I

Name and Purpose

Section 1. The name of this association shall be the Bel Air Shopping City Merchants Association.

Section 2. Bel Air Shopping City Merchants Association is incorporated for the advancement of commercial and civic interests of the Bel Air Shopping City, and in furtherance of such object to engage in and conduct all possible promotional activity, to seek publicity, conduct special events, organize cooperative advertising, and other joint endeavors in the general interest and for the general benefit of all merchants in the center which is located in Asheville, North Carolina.

Section 3. All actions in the conduct of Association business by its officers, directors, and employees shall be subject to the control of the Association Membership. The General Membership delegates to the Board of Directors the responsibility for implementing the objectives of the group as detailed in these Bylaws and by policy decisions of the Membership. The Membership shall have the right and authority to pass upon the annual budget and to develop and define the limits within which the Association shall function.

Article II

Membership

Section 1. There shall be two types of membership: General and Affiliate.

Section 2. General Membership. General Member is a person or a company maintaining a place of business within the limits of Bel Air Shopping City. A representative of the developer shall also maintain General Membership. Each such member shall be entitled to one vote, notwithstanding the size of such member's business or assessment.

Section 3. Affiliate Membership. An Affiliate Member is a person or a company who has been admitted to the Association by vote of members upon recommendation of the Board of Directors of the Association. He shall have voice at meetings, but shall not be permitted to vote, and shall be excused from attendance at any meeting or portion thereof, when said meeting shall go into executive session. (Such affiliate member might be an attorney, a maintenance firm, an accountant, or other such individuals.)

Article III

Dues

Section 1. There shall be an annual assessment to be paid by each General Member of the Association. This assessment will be determined by the Board of Directors on the basis of each individual tenant's space occupancy as related to the total footage, with proportionate adjustments in rate for members occupying more than one floor, or the nature of whose businesses or services might, in the opinion of the Directors, justify a rate lower than the basic assessment formula.

The above assessment will constitute that member's annual dues, and such assessment shall be paid in one billing, semiannual billing, quarter-annual billing, or monthly billing, to be decided by the General Membership.

Section 2. Whenever a member shall be in arrears in payment of his annual dues for more than ninety (90) days, he shall be notified in writing that if he does not pay them within 14 days of the postmarked date, he shall be deemed a delinquent member and reported to the Bel Air Shopping City management as being delinquent and in violation of his lease.

Section 3. Such a delinquent member shall not be entitled to vote and shall be removed from any office he may then be occupying.

Section 4. Members not paying invoices for cooperative advertising within thirty (30) days after billing date shall be considered delinquent, and excluded from further joint promotions until their accounts are current.

Section 5. A member of the Board of Directors shall be removed after three (3) unexcused absences within one fiscal year.

Article IV

Board of Directors

Section 1. The Board of Directors of the Association shall consist of one representative from each of the major stores: Collins Bros., Moss & Browne, Lee-Spencer, and Kor-Mart as well as a designee from Bel Air Shopping City. A minimum of six (6) other members which may be expanded to a maximum of ten (10), are to be elected by the General Membership. The representative of Bel Air Shopping City shall not be eligible to hold office.

Section 2. Of the six (6) to ten (10) to be elected by the membership, one-half (½) shall be elected for a two (2) year period and the remaining one-half (½) shall be elected for a one (1) year period.

Section 3. The Board of Directors shall have authority and responsibility to implement the objectives of the Association to the best of their ability, making such policy decision as may be necessary and proper to accomplish this within the framework of the Bylaws.

Section 4. The Management of the Association and the control of the Association's property shall be vested in the Board of Directors.

Section 5. Meetings of the Board of Directors shall be held at the call of the President of the Association or by written request of the majority of the Board of Directors, but in no event shall be less than once each month. There shall be quarterly meetings of the entire membership in January, April, July, and October.

Section 6. The President of the Association shall be the Director of the Board, and the Secretary of the Association shall be the Secretary of the Board.

Section 7. A majority of the Board of Directors shall constitute a quorum for the transaction of business at any regular or special meeting of the Board.

Article V

Officers

Section 1. Officers of this Association shall consist of a President, Vice-President, Treasurer, and Secretary, who shall be elected by the Board of Directors at their first meeting following the January meeting of the General Membership, for a term of one year, commencing February 1st, and each shall serve until his successor has been duly elected and qualified for office.

Section 2. The President shall preside at all meetings of the Association and shall be the Chief Executive Officer of the Association. He shall also be an ex-officio member of all committees.

Section 3. The Vice-President shall act for the President in the event of his absence or disability, and shall succeed to the office of President if a vacancy should occur in that office.

Section 4. The Treasurer shall be the collector and custodian of all Association funds and shall keep true and accurate accounts with respect to all financial transactions of the Association and shall render a financial report at each quarterly meeting of the Association. All checks issued by the Association shall be signed by the President and countersigned by the Treasurer. In the absence of either or both,

two (2) other officers of the Association shall sign checks. The Treasurer shall be bonded in the amount of $75,000.

Section 5. The Secretary shall keep all the records of the Association except the financial records, shall act as custodian of its corporate seal, and shall attest all acts of the Association and shall perform such other duties as may be necessary and proper in the connection with said office. (Secretary may, with permission of Board, appoint an assistant.)

Article VI

Committees

Section 1. There shall be an Executive Committee of 5, consisting of the President, Vice-President, and Secretary, with two other Directors elected by the Board. This Executive Committee, during the time between meetings of the Board of Directors, shall have and exercise all the powers granted to the Board of Directors in the management and direction of the affairs of the Association, but shall not in any way conflict with specific directions as shall have been given by the Board of Directors, or with these Bylaws. All actions of the Executive Committee shall be reported at the next meeting of the Board of Directors succeeding such action, and may thereupon be subject to revision, alteration, or cancellation by majority vote of the Board of Directors, provided the rights of third parties shall not be affected thereby. A majority of the Executive Committee shall be necessary to constitute a quorum and the affirmative vote of the majority of the members of the Executive Committee shall be necessary to the adoption of any resolution or action of the Executive Committee. The Executive Committee shall not be empowered to initiate assessments or expenditures to be effective before such assessments or expenditures are approved by the Board of Directors.

Section 2. There shall be a nominations committee consisting of seven (7) members appointed by the President at the October quarterly meeting preceding the annual meeting. The nominations committee shall submit in writing its nominations for directors to be elected. These nominations shall be made within thirty (30) days after the committee has been designated and voting shall be at the quarterly meeting in January. Notice of said nominations shall be mailed to the membership at least ten (10) days prior to the election.

Nominations for Directors may also be made by the petition of five (5) members of the Association, said nominations to be filed with the Secretary of the Association at least three (3) days prior to the election meeting.

Section 3. The President shall appoint the members of all the committees, subject to approval of the Board of Directors, except as otherwise herein provided.

Section 4. No committee or individual shall represent the Association, in support of or in opposition to any project or thing without the specific authorization of the Board of Directors. Neither shall any committee or individual incur any financial obligation for or on behalf of the Association beyond the scope of authority of such committee or individual as duly authorized by the annual budget without authorization from the Board of Directors.

Article VII

Meetings, Vacancies and Removals

Section 1. The Association shall meet regularly on the first Wednesday of each fiscal quarter: February, May, August, and November. Special meetings may be called by the President, the Board of Directors, or on petition of twenty-five (25%) percent of the membership of the Association.

Section 2. Each member shall be mailed notice of all meetings to his last listed address shown on Association records. Said notices shall reach at least 3 days before each meeting.

Section 3. A member who is a firm may vote through an employee of the firm.

Section 4. One-quarter (¼) of the total membership of the Association in good standing shall constitute a quorum for the transaction of business at any regular or special meeting. All meetings shall be conducted in accordance with Robert's Rules of Order, latest revised edition.

Section 5. All vacancies in the Board of Directors or of any other office of the Association shall be filled by a majority vote of the Board of Directors.

Section 6. Any member of the Board, any officer of the Association, or any member of the Association may be removed from such office or membership by a two-thirds (2/3) vote of those attending a regular meeting or a special meeting of the Association called for such purpose, providing that a quorum is present.

Article VIII

Audit of Books

Section 1. The books of the Association shall be audited annually by a certified public accountant, to be chosen by the Board of Directors. He shall render his report to the general membership at the February meeting.

Article IX

Fiscal Year

Section 1. The fiscal year of the Association shall begin annually on February 1 and end on January 31st.

Article X

Amendments

Section 1. Proposed amendments to the Bylaws shall be presented in writing, to the Secretary of the Association. A notice of such proposed amendment and copy thereof shall be mailed to all members of the Association at least five (5) days prior to the date of the meeting at which the Amendment is to be considered. An affirmative vote of a majority of the Board of Directors of the Association shall be necessary to adopt any amendment.

Merchants Association Bylaws III

Article I

Definitions

SECTION 1. The following terms shall have these meanings wherever used in these Bylaws:

"Association" denotes Bel Air Shopping City Merchants Association, Inc.

"Shopping City Area" refers to these parcels of land in Asheville, Fayette County, North Carolina, consisting of Parcels 17, 18, 19, 20, 21, and 22 as recorded among the Land Records of Fayette County in Plot Book 6, Page 61. Additional plots in the same Fayette County, Asheville, North Carolina designated as Parcels 23, 24, 25 are duly recorded among the Fayette County, Asheville, North Carolina Land Records in Plot Book 6, Page 62. These additional plots of land shall be referred to as the "Shopping City Parking Area."

SECTION 2. "Opening Period" shall designate the time commencing with the preopening promotion and advertising relating to the Grand Opening of the Shopping City and continuing thirty (30) days after the Grand Opening. "Grand Opening" shall mean the date established by the Bel Air City Management as the date the Shopping City shall officially open for business and such "Grand Opening" shall be participated in by a minimum of two (2) Department (Anchor) Stores and at least one-third (⅓) of those retail and service establishments with Bel Air Shopping City leases. Such "Grand Opening" shall be deferred until the minimum participation quotes are met.

SECTION 3. "Association Year" shall denote successive periods of twelve (12) months starting with termination of the "Opening Period."

Article II

Objectives, Members, Dues, and Assessments

SECTION 1—Objectives. The purpose of the Association shall be to promote, develop and increase the flow of traffic to Bel Air Shopping City and to participate in community and civic activities and in developing such objectives, to plan and pursue cooperative advertising, traffic-building "devices," special community-interest events, and any cohesive programs for the general benefit of merchants in the "Shopping City Area." The Association shall be conducted as a nonprofit organization, and no part of the profits (if any) of the Association shall inure to the benefit of any member, person, firm, or corporation.

SECTION 2—Members. All occupants of retail, service, and other space in the "Shopping City Area" as required by lease or other form of agreement with Bel Air Shopping City, Inc., to become members of the Merchants Association shall join the Association and contribute the sums as provided in their respective leases, or agreements. From the formation of the Association until the end of the first Association Year, each member shall be entitled to one vote for each dollar assessed by the Association against such member for the First Year. During each Association Year thereafter, each member shall again be entitled to one vote for each dollar assessed by the Association against such member for the upcoming Association Year. There shall be only one (1) class of members and Bel Air Shopping City, Inc., and its successors in ownership to any part of the Shopping City Area shall join and remain members of the Association and shall have the right and privilege to attend all meetings of the Association and to participate in its activities.

SECTION 3—Assessments. Assessments shall be paid by all members of the Association as provided for under the respective lease or other agreement between each such member and Bel Air Shopping City, Inc., or its successor or successors in ownership.

No member of the Association obligated to pay any assessment under its respective lease or other agreement with Bel Air Shopping City, Inc., shall be required to pay an assessment in excess of the amount provided in said lease or other agreement, unless special assessments are voted by a two-thirds (2/3) majority of the Association Membership or on a voluntary request basis. Bel Air Shopping City, Inc., shall pay an annual assessment of not less than one-quarter (¼) of the total annual aggregate contribution of other members of the Assocation under the terms of their respective leases and other agreements with Bel Air Shopping City, Inc. They shall also pay not less than one-quarter (¼) of the aggregate sum contributed by all other Association Members because of special or voluntary assessments. All assessments shall be payable within ten (10) days after billing by the Association.

SECTION 4—Annual Meetings. The Association shall hold an annual meeting of the members for the purpose of election of Directors and Officers, approval of the Association budget, and to transact any other business properly brought before the Association. The first annual meeting of the Association will be held on Wednesday, October 1, 19xx with subsequent annual meetings to be held on the first Wednesday of October.

Any proper business of the Association may be transacted at any annual meeting without being specifically required by the Articles of Incorporation to be stated in the meeting notice. Failure to hold an annual meeting at the designated time shall not invalidate the corporate existence of the Association or affect otherwise valid acts permitted by the Articles of Incorporation.

SECTION 5—Association Meetings. At any time during the period between annual meetings, but with not less than seven (7) days notice, special meetings of the members may be called by the President, by a majority of the Board of Directors, or any twelve (12) members of the Association by submitting a request in writing to the Secretary with a copy of the notice of meeting as required by Section 7.

SECTION 6—Place of Meetings. All meetings of the members shall be held at the principal office of the Association in the Shopping City Area, except when the notices for the meetings shall designate another place; however, all meetings, both regular and special, shall be held within Fayette County, North Carolina.

SECTION 7—Notice of Meetings. Not less than seven (7) days, nor more than thirty (30) days before the date of every annual or special meeting of members, the Secretary shall give to each member in good standing written notice, by mail, personal delivery, or by leaving it at his usual place of business, stating the time and place of the meeting and, in the case of a special meeting, by whom and the purposes for which the meeting is called. If mailed, such notice shall be deemed to be given when deposited with prepaid postage and addressed to the member at his post office address as it appears on the records of the Association. Notwithstanding the foregoing provision, a waiver of notice in writing, signed by the Association Members entitled to such notice and filed with the records of the meeting, whether before or after it is held, or actual attendance at the meeting in person or by proxy, shall be deemed equivalent to the giving of such meeting notice to such persons entitled thereto. Any meeting, annual or special, of members may adjourn from time to time to reconvene at the same or some other place, and no additional notice need be given of such adjourned meeting other than by announcement of the postponement, the rescheduled date, time, and place.

SECTION 8—Quorum. At any annual or special meeting of members, the presence in person or by proxy of members entitled to cast majority of all the votes shall constitute a quorum. In the absence of a quorum, the members present in person or by proxy, by majority vote and without notice other than by announcement, may adjourn the meeting from time to time until a quorum shall attend. At any such adjourned meeting at which a quorum shall be present, any business may be transacted which might have been transacted at the meeting as originally notified.

SECTION 9—Votes Required. A majority of the votes cast at any duly called meeting of members, at which a quorum is present and voting, shall be sufficient to take or authorize action upon any matter which may properly come before the meeting, unless more than a majority of votes cast is required by the Articles of Incorporation or by these Bylaws.

SECTION 10—Proxies. Any member may vote either in person or by written proxy, or a duly designated representative may cast the ballot if authorized in writing by such member.

SECTION 11—Voting. For purposes of electing Directors at all annual meetings, each member shall have the right to vote for as many persons as there are Directors to be elected. Unless so demanded by any member, voting need not be by ballot, nor be conducted by inspectors.

SECTION 12—Assessment Delinquency. Any member who shall be in arrears in the payment of assessments for more than thirty (30) days shall not be entitled to vote on any matter or election before the Association.

Article III

Board of Directors

SECTION 1—Powers. The business and all related affairs of the Association shall be managed by its Board of Directors. The Board of Directors may exercise all the powers of the Association except such as are by the Articles of Incorporation or the Bylaws specifically reserved to the members. The Board of Directors shall keep detailed and accurate records of all its transactions.

SECTION 2—Number of Directors. There shall be no less than eleven (11), nor more than seventeen (17), Directors of the Association elected from among Association members or their duly designated representatives: one (1) of whom shall be an employee of Collins Bros., one (1) of whom shall be an employee of Moss and Browne, one (1) of whom shall be an employee of Lee-Spencer, and one (1) of whom shall be named by Kor-mart. Bel Air Shop-

ping City, Inc., shall also name one (1) Director to represent management.

SECTION 3—Election of Directors. Until the first annual meeting of the Association or until successors are duly elected and qualify, the Board of Directors shall consist of the persons named as such in the Articles of Incorporation of the Association. At the first annual meeting of the Association and at each annual meeting thereafter, the members shall elect Directors, in the number and composition stipulated in Article III, Section 2, to hold office until the next succeeding annual meeting or until their successors are elected and qualified.

SECTION 4—Vacancies. Should a vacancy occur on the Board of Directors for any cause other than by reason of an increase in the number of Directors, the vacancy shall remain unfilled until the next annual election if the number of Directors are at, or above, the eleven (11) minimum level; otherwise a new Director is named by a majority of the remaining Directors. Any vacancy occurring by reason of an increase in the number of Directors may be filled only by action of a majority of the entire Board of Directors. A Director designated to fill a vacancy shall hold office until the next annual meeting of members or until his successor is elected and qualified by special meeting.

SECTION 5—Regular Meetings. Regular meetings of the Board of Directors shall be held on such dates and at such places within Fayette County, North Carolina, as may be designated from time to time by the Board of Directors.

SECTION 6—Special Meetings. Special meetings of the Board of Directors may be called at any time by the President, by a majority of the Board of Directors, by majority vote of members at an annual or special meeting. Such special meetings shall be held at such locale, or locales, within Fayette County, North Carolina, as may be designated by the Board of Directors. In the absence of such designation, meetings shall be held at the regular meeting place in Bel Air Shopping City.

SECTION 7—Notice of Meetings. Except as otherwise provided in this Section, notice of the place, day, and hour of every regular and special meeting of the Board of Directors shall be given to each Director at least three (3) business working days preceding the proposed meeting, by delivering such notice to him personally, or by sending the same to him by telegraph, or by leaving notice at his usual place of business, or as the alternative, by mailing such notice four (4) days before the proposed meeting, postage prepaid, and addressed to him at his last known Post Office address shown on the records of the Association. Unless required by these Bylaws or by resolution of the Board of Directors, no notice of any meeting of the Board of Directors need state the business to be transacted at that meeting. No notice of any meeting of the Board of Directors need be given to any Director who actually attends, or to any Director who, in writing, files with the records of the meeting either before or after the holding thereof, waivers of such notice. Any meeting of the Board of Directors, regular or special, may adjourn from time to time to reconvene at the same or some other place, and no notice need be given of any such adjourned meeting other than by announcement of the rescheduled meeting date, time, and place.

SECTION 8—Quorum. At all meetings of the Board of Directors, a majority of the entire Board of Trustees shall constitute a quorum for the transaction of business. Except in cases in which it is by the Articles of Incorporation of the Association or by the Bylaws otherwise provided, the vote of a majority of those Directors present at a duly constituted meeting, at which a quorum is present and voting, shall be sufficient to elect and pass any measure. In the absence of such quorum, the Directors present by majority vote and without notice other than by announcement may adjourn the meeting from time to time until a quorum shall be in attendance. At any such adjourned meeting at which a quorum shall be present, any business may be transacted which might have been transacted at the meeting as originally notified.

Article IV

Officers

SECTION 1—Executive Officers. Subsequent to the first annual meeting of the Association and immediately following every annual meeting thereafter the Board of Directors shall elect from among their number a President, a Vice-President, a Secretary, and a Treasurer of the Merchants Association. Any vacancy occurring in any of the above offices may be filled by the Board of Directors at any regular or special meeting and each such officer shall hold office until his successor is elected and qualified. The Board of Directors may designate one (1) Assistant Secretary and one (1) Assistant Treasurer, neither of whom may be a Director, nor be entitled to a vote, but may attend Directors' meetings ex-officio. Any two (2) of the offices of the Association, except those of President and Vice-President, may be held by the same person at the same time but no officer shall execute, acknowledge, or verify any contract or agreement in more than one (1) capacity if such instrument be required by the Articles of Incorporation of the Association, by these Bylaws, or by resolution of the Board of Directors to be executed, acknowledged, or verified by any two (2) or more officers. Each officer shall hold office until the newly elected Board of Directors meets immediately following each annual meeting of the Association for purposes of electing new officers of the Association, or until said officer resigns, or until said officer's successor shall have been duly elected and qualified.

SECTION 2—President. The President shall preside at all meetings of the members of the Association and of the Board of Directors at which he shall be present; he shall have general charge and supervision of the business of the Association; he may sign and execute, in the name of the Association, all authorized deeds, mortgages, bonds, contracts, or other instruments except in cases in which the signing and execution thereof have been expressly delegated to some other officer or agent of the Association by the Articles of Incorporation of the Association or these Bylaws; and, in general, he shall perform all duties incident to the office of a President of a Corporation, and such other duties as, from time to time, may be assigned to him by the Board of Directors.

SECTION 3— Vice-President. The Vice-President, at the request of the President or in his absence or during his inability to act, shall perform the duties and exercise the functions of the President, and when so acting shall have the powers of the President. The Vice-President shall have such other powers and perform such other duties as may be assigned to him by the Board of Directors or the President.

SECTION 4—Secretary. The Secretary shall keep the minutes of all meetings of the members of the Association and the Board of Directors in books provided for that purpose; he shall see that all notices are given and delivered in accordance with the provisions of these Bylaws or as required by law; he shall see that the corporate seal is affixed to all documents the execution of which, on behalf of the Association, under its seal, is duly authorized, when so affixed may attest the same; he shall be custodian of all records of the Association; and, in general, he shall perform all duties incident to the office of a Secretary of a Corporation, and such other duties, as from time to time, may be assigned to him by the President or Board of Directors.

SECTION 5—Treasurer. The Treasurer shall have charge of, and be responsible and accountable for, all funds, securities, receipts, and disbursements of the Association, and shall deposit, or cause to be deposited, in the name of the Association, all monies or other assets in such banks, trust companies, or other depositories as shall, from time to time, be selected by the Board of Directors; he shall render to the President and to the Board of Directors, whenever requested, an account of the financial condition of the Association; and, in general, he shall perform all duties incident to the office of a Treasurer of a Corporation, and such other duties as may be assigned to him by the Board of Directors or the President.

SECTION 6—Assistant Officers. The Assistant Secretary shall have such duties as may, from time to time, be assigned to him by the Secretary. The Assistant Treasurer shall have such duties, as may, from time to time, be assigned to him by the Treasurer.

SECTION 7—Subordinate Officers. The Board of Directors may, during their tenure, appoint such subordinate officers as it may deem necessary. Each such subordinate officer shall hold office at the pleasure of the Board of Directors and shall perform such duties as the Board of Directors or the President may designate. The Board of Directors may, as deemed necessary, authorize any committee or officer to appoint or remove subordinate officers and detail the duties thereof.

SECTION 8—Removal. Any officer or agent of the Association may be removed by majority vote of the Board of Directors whenever, in its judgment, the best interest of the Association will be served by this action.

Article V

Sundry Provisions

SECTION 1—Checks, Drafts, Etc. All checks, drafts and orders for payment of money, notes and other other evidences of indebtedness, issued in the name of the Association, shall, unless otherwise provided by resolution of the Board of Directors, be signed by the President or, if he is not available, by the Vice-President; also to be countersigned by the Treasurer or the Secretary in his absence. The Treasurer shall be bonded to the extent prescribed by the Board of Directors.

SECTION 2—Annual Reports. There shall be prepared annually a complete and accurate statement of the affairs of the Association, including a financial statement of operations for the preceding calendar year, to be prepared by and certified to by a qualified accountant who is not a member of the Association.

SECTION 3—Proposed Budget. The Treasurer shall prepare, in conjunction with the Board of Directors, a proposed budget for the next Association year and present, copy of same to each Association member at the annual meeting.

SECTION 4—Business. The business year of the Association shall be the "Association Year," unless otherwise provided by the Board of Directors.

SECTION 5—Seal. The Board of Directors

shall provide a suitable seal, bearing the name of the Association, which shall be in the charge of the Secretary. The Board of Directors may authorize one (1) or more duplicate seals and provide for the custody thereof.

SECTION 6—Debts. The Association shall not incur debts for the individual members under any circumstances.

SECTION 7—Amendments. Any and all provisions of these Bylaws may be altered or repealed, and new Bylaws may be adopted by a vote of not less than sixty-six and two-thirds percent (66 2/3%) of votes eligible to be cast at any annual meeting of the members, or at any special meeting called for that purpose.

SECTION 8—Rules of Procedure. Except as otherwise provided in these Bylaws, the Association shall be governed by, and all meetings conducted in accordance with, the rules contained in "Robert's Rules of Order, Revised."

Grand Opening Assessment Notification

TO: BEL AIR SHOPPING CENTER TENANTS

FROM: AARON B. MOSIER, BEL AIR SHOPPING CITY PROJECT DIRECTOR

RE: GRAND OPENING PROMOTION

PHASE I of the Bel Air Shopping City Grand Opening promotion is now realistically planned for Thursday, October 4, 19xx. At that time, 79 of a total of 114 tenants, including 3 out of 4 department stores, will open for business.

Two important items that will favorably affect and contribute to a successful Grand Opening are the excellent timing and the fact that more than two-thirds (⅔) of the total tenant population will be opening on Thursday, October 4, 19xx. I am sure we are all in agreement that an exciting, productive Grand Opening will give Bel Air Shopping City the momentum that is so vital during this period. A strong, well-publicized, highly promotional Grand Opening will provide the platform for continuing high-customer traffic and accelerating dollar volume.

The other component, of equal importance to the timing and the number of merchants opening on October 4, is adequate funding of the Grand Opening promotion. Most shopping center leases now provide for this contingency, which is, of course, a part of the agreement with Bel Air Shopping City tenants. In addition, a lease clause and the Merchants Association Bylaws provide for complete tenant support of Center-sponsored advertising and promotion during both the Grand Opening period and on a continuing basis after the center has opened.

Your Grand Opening assessment, as defined by lease, is 20¢ per square foot. This totals to the dollar amount shown above, and is one half (½) of your annual dues. All department stores are making substantial contributions to the opening promotion and advertising fund, in addition to impressive expenditures of their own, that will be coordinated with Bel Air Shopping City promotion.

Recognizing the importance of the Grand Opening, your landlord-developer will contribute one-third (⅓) of the total merchant amount, instead of the 25 percent (25%) mandated by lease. However, after the Grand Opening period, the amount will revert to the stipulated 25 percent (25%).

All contributions are for the Preopening, opening, and first 30-day promotion, and a copy of the budget which details these expenditures is attached hereto. You will shortly receive an invoice for your assessment in the amount shown. Will you please forward your check as soon as possible after its receipt, so funds will be available, and we may proceed with the Grand Opening promotional program as detailed on the plans.

You will be kept fully informed about the progress of the Grand Opening promotion as it develops.

Fact Sheet

Project Name Bel Air Shopping City

Location: N.C. Highway 28

Opening Date: Thursday, October 4, 19xx.

Gross Leasable Area (including 4 Majors):
1,200,000 sq. ft.

Tenant Capacity (Including 4 Majors):
114 stores

Thursday, October 4, 19xx Opening:
840,000 sq. ft.

Thursday, October 4, Tenant Occupancy (Including 3 Majors):
79 stores

Major Access Highways:
U.S. 95 and N.C. 280—N.C. 280 now rebuilding into four (4) lane
highway. Completion target date October 1, 19xx.

Population in Primary and Secondary Trading Areas:
641,703. Projected yearly growth plan—3.4%

Average Family Income in Primary and Secondary Markets:
$12,642 annually

Project Director:
Franklin Development Corporation—Aaron B. Mosier

Construction Supervisor:
Franklin Development Corporation—George E. Quinn

Planning and Design Director:
Franklin Development Corporation—Donald G. Klein

Landscape Planning:
Franklin Development Corporation, Santori Landscaping Co.—Antonio Santori

Leasing Executives:
Franklin Development Corporation—Donald E. Brooks; Joseph F. Schilling

Center Manager:
Earl Gordon

Promotion and Advertising Agency:
Ace Advertising, Inc.

Promotion Director:
George Hixson

General Contractor:
Seaboldt—Moore Construction Co., Inc.

Engineers:
Fallon—Dolan Engineering, Inc.

Grand Openings:
Phase I. Thursday, October 4, 19xx—79 stores including 3 majors
Phase II. Thursday, March 6, 19xx—35 stores including 1 major

Suggested Use of Logo-Type

Various sizes of the complete logo for Bel Air Shopping City are included in this brochure.

All merchants are hereby requested to use this material adjacent to, immediately above, or below their store name in newspaper advertisements, circulars, mailers, or any other print media advertising their products or services.

While this is not mandatory by lease agreement, utilization of the logo-type by all advertisers in Bel Air Shopping City Merchants Association sponsored special sections, mailers, or circulars will provide the uniform look necessary to promote the Center as a single entity. Cover or lead pages as well as banners will always use the logo in conjunction with the address: "U.S. 95 at Exit 9."

It is further suggested that "run-of-the-paper" (non-Center sponsored) advertising use the Bel Air Shopping City Logo-type in their individual ads for continuing emphasis and identification.

Preopening, Opening, and First 30 Day Budget Summary

I Print
A. Space $11,753
B. Production 1,900
Total Newspapers $13,653

II Electronics
A. Time
  1. Radio .... $ 8,676
  2. Television 6,360
B. Production 2,625
Total Electronics $17,661

III Publicity .... $ 4,175
IV Brochures 2,550
V Special Events 6,294
VI Administration 17,834
VII Agency 3,276
VIII Insurance 750
IX Donations 1,500
X Contingency 3,500
Total Items III Thru X 39,879
Budget Brand Total $71,193

I. PRINT

A 86″ "Teaser" ad—Sunday, September 9th—*Citizen, Times* $903

B 86″ "Teaser" ad—Sunday, September 16th—*Citizen, Times* $903

C 43″ "Teaser" ad—Wednesday P.M., September 19th—*Times* $194

D 43″ "Teaser" ad—Thursday A.M., September 20th—*Citizen* $322

E 86″ "Teaser" ad—Sunday, September 23rd—*Citizen, Times* $903

F 43″ "Teaser" ad—Wednesday P.M., September 26th—*Times* $194

G 43″ "Teaser" ad—Thursday A.M., September 27th—*Citizen* $322

H 172″ Preopening announcement ad—Sunday, September 30th—*Citizen, Times* $1,806

I 172″ Preopening announcement ad—Monday P.M., October 1st—*Times* $774

J 172″ Preopening announcement ad—Tuesday A.M., October 2nd—*Citizen* $1,290

K 172″ Special Opening Section (Merchants Association cost for cover page) Wednesday P.M., October 3rd—*Times* $774

L 172″ Special Opening Section (Merchants Association cost for cover page) Thursday A.M., October 4th—*Citizen* $1,290

M 86″ Institutional ad—Friday P.M., October 5th—*Times* $387

N 86″ Columbus Day ad—Sunday, October 7th—*Citizen, Times* $903

O 75″ Tabloid Section (Merchants Association cost for cover page) Sunday, October 21st— *Citizen, Times* $788

A. Total Space Cost $11,753

B. Production Cost $1,900

Total Newspaper Cost $13,653

II. ELECTRONICS

1. RADIO
Week Beginning Sunday, September 9th

40 spots, W A V J	$360
40 spots, W A B D	420
	$780

Week Beginning Sunday, September 18th

48 spots, W A V J	$432
48 spots, W A B D	504
40 spots, W A C L	480
	$1,416

Week Beginning Sunday, September 23rd

70 spots, W A V L	$630
60 spots, W A B D	630
48 spots, W A C L	576
	$1,836

Week Beginning Sunday, September 30th (Opening)

100 spots, W A V L	$900
100 spots, W A B D	1,050
80 spots, W A C L	960
	$2,910

Week Beginning Sunday, October 7th

50 spots, W A V J	$450
48 spots, W A B D	504
	$954

Week Beginning Sunday, October 14th

40 spots, W A V J	$360
40 spots, W A B D	420
	$780

Total Radio $8,676

2. TELEVISION
Week Beginning Sunday, September 9th

W C A V, 5 spots	....	$300
W A R V, 5 spots	....	225
		$525

Week Beginning Sunday, September 16th

W C A V, 7 spots	....	$420
W A R V, 7 spots	....	315
		$735

Week Beginning Sunday, September 23rd

W C A V, 15 spots	....	$900
W A R V, 10 spots	....	450
		$1,350

Week Beginning Sunday, September 30th (Opening)

W C A V, 30 spots	....	$1,800
W A R V, 20 spots	....	900
		$2,700

Week Beginning Sunday, October 7th

W C A V, 5 spots	....	$300
W A R V, 5 spots	....	225
		$525

Week Beginning Sunday, October 21st

W C A V, 5 spots	....	$300
W A R V, 5 spots	....	225
		$525

Total Television Cost	....	$6,360
Total Radio Cost	....	$8,676
Production (Radio and Television) Costs	....	$2,625
Total Electronics Cost	....	$17,661

III. PUBLICITY

A Ribbon Cutting Ceremony	....	$ 425
B Celebrity Appearance	....	2,000
C Loudspeaker Cars	....	525
D Band	....	500
E Leaflets	....	475
F Miscellaneous	....	250
Total	....	4,175

IV. BROCHURES $2,550
V. SPECIAL EVENTS $6,294

Fund to be used for traffic-building activities during opening and 30-day period following center opening—details to follow.

VI. ADMINISTRATION (See Summary) 17,834
VII. AGENCY 3,276
VIII. INSURANCE 750
IX. DONATIONS 1,500
X. CONTINGENCY .... $ 3,500

Summary of Administration Costs

Preopening, Opening, and First 30 Days

Promotion Director Salary (for above period) .... $ 8,000
Secretary Salary (for above period) 4,000
Total $12,000

Office Equipment:
Typewriter and Mimeo $1,800
Stationery 1,350
Petty Cash 900
Telephone 950
Misc 834
Total 5,834
GRAND TOTAL $17,834

APPENDIX C

Notification of Annual Membership Meeting

DATE: September 5, 19xx

TO: All Principals and Managers

FROM: George Hixson—Bel Air Shopping City Merchants Association

SUBJECT: Annual Membership Meeting

Meeting Time, Place, Date:
A Merchants Association meeting with the General Membership will be held on Wednesday, October 1, 19xx in the Coach Room of the Red Lion Inn, intersection of Routes 280 and 95 in Asheville, North Carolina. The business meeting will start at 6:00 P.M. sharp, preceded by a 5:30 P.M. to 6:30 P.M. cocktail hour, and a dinner starting at 6:30 P.M.

Meeting Objectives:
• Election of a slate of Directors* to serve for the next year in accordance with the Bylaws of this Association. Officers shall be elected by the new Board from among their numbers immediately following this meeting.

• Annual Budget—presentation, discussion, and vote by General Membership.

• Any other business requiring General Membership approval as mandated in the Bylaws.

*If operating with a Promotion Fund, substitute: "Selection of the Steering Committee."

Directions to Red Lion Inn:
Detailed map attached. Driving time from downtown Asheville, 25 minutes. From Asheville-Hendersonville airport to Red Lion Inn, 35 minutes.

R.S.V.P. Merchants Association Meeting:
Please return the enclosed RSVP sheet, naming your store representative(s) who will attend. There will be a charge of twelve (12) dollars for cocktails and dinner for each additional person, over and above the two allotted to every Merchants Association member. One or more of your representatives shall have the authority to vote on all agenda items.

Enclosed Information:
A sample ballot is enclosed herewith. This is a facsimile of the one that will be used for the election of the Board of Directors and inclusion of other nominations from the floor. A review is suggested prior to this meeting, at which time official ballots will be distributed for your vote on the nominees for the Board of Directors. The Annual Budget and other matters requiring general membership approval will be handled by voice vote or a show of hands. (Delete this paragraph if operating with a promotion fund).

We hope that you will review this information and give it your careful attention in advance. Your cooperation in arranging your schedule to attend this very important meeting will be appreciated by Management as well as your incumbent Directors and Officers. Your presence will give you and your company voice in the operation and decisions of your Merchants Association during this upcoming year. (If operating with a promotion fund, substitute a paragraph relating to the Steering Committee).

Merchants Association
(Do not include if promotion fund operation.) The attached ballot is for election of a Board of Directors as specified in Article III, Section 2 and 3 of the Bel Air Shopping City Merchants Association Bylaws.

Barry Williams, Barbara Langley, and Bruce Kamron have served as the nominating committee and respectfully submit the attached list of ten (10) candidates for election to the Board of Directors of the Bel Air Shopping City. A total of six (6) shall be elected from among their number, with the remaining five (5) seats to be filled by permanent members of the Board of Directors as specified in Article III, Section 2 of the Bylaws. The five (5) nonelective Directors are listed on the ballot and indicated with an (X).

Please vote for the remaining six (6) by placing an (X) in the block beside their names, or for any other candidate(s) nominated from the floor whose name(s) is to be entered in the space provided for write-in candidates. Your vote for both listed and write-in candidates is not to exceed six (6).

Officers will be elected by the new Board of Directors from among their number immediately following this meeting.

Merchants Association Board of Directors Election

Vote for Six (6) Candidates Only (Do not include if Promotion Fund operational)

Declared Candidates		Permanent Directors	
1. Joseph Mangoff, I. Worth & Co.		Collins Bros.	X
2. Peter Griffen, Modern Jeweler		Moss and Browne	X
3. Samuel Iderson, Built-Rite Shoes		Lee Spencer	X
4. Lily Atkins, Manger Co.		Kor-Mart	X
5. Keith Leonards, Area Manager		Bel Air Shopping City	X
6. Sarah Leventhal, Casual Fashion			
7. Gerald Frenzer, Child-Togs			
8. William Karter, Sports World			
9. Leon Penerson, Food Mart			
10. Penny Soroff, Lee's Fashions			
Write-in Candidates			

Annual Budget

November 1, 19XX Through October 31, 19XX

I. Print

 A. Space $23,646
 B. Production 3,160
 Total Newspapers $26,806

II. Electronics
 A. Time
  1. Radio $19,644
  2. Television 13,827
 B. Production 4,592
 Total Electronics $38,063

III. Publicity .... $ 7,333
IV. Brochures 2,666
V. Special Events 11,843
VI. Administration 34,667
VII. Agency 6,000
VIII. Insurance 3,333
IX. Donations 3,333
X. Contingency 8,000
Total Budget $142,044

SUMMARY OF

ITEM	COST
Total Promotional Events Cost	$ 76,712
Publicity	7,333
Brochures	2,666
Administration	34,667
Agency	6,000
Insurance	3,333
Donations	3,333
Contingency	8,000
Total	$142,044

Annual Budget Breakdown

EVENT	PROMOTION DATE(S)	PRINT	RADIO	T.V.	EVENTS ON THE MALL	COMMENTS
Election Day Specials	Nov. 6th	$1,200	$ 880	$ 720	$400—Election Information Booth	One-Day Election Day Event Only
Pre-Christmas	Nov. 15th	$2,501	$1,635	$1,307	$9,000—Decorations $520—Santa Arrives	Newspaper ad Thanksgiving Day, Radio and T.V., Thurs., Fri., Sat.
Christmas	Beg. Nov. 23rd	$2,434	$2,123	$1,307		Regular priced advertising
After Christmas Clearance	Dec. 26th	$1,489	$1,293	$1,030	$667—To be Scheduled	Sale event starts day after Christmas. Newspaper ad Christmas Day or Dec. 26th. Radio and T.V. beginning Christmas Day through Saturday
January Sidewalk Sale	Jan. 24th, 25th, 26th	$ 713	$ 880	$ 687	$667—Booths	Three-Day Event
Washington's Birthday Sale	Feb. 16th, 17th, 18th	$1,489	$1,702	$ 967	$534—Meet George and Martha Washington	Fri., Sat., and Mon Sale Event
Spring Fashion Fling	Mar. 6th, 7th, 8th	$1,243	$ 880	$ 720	$534—Flower Show	Three-Day Sale Event
Easter	Beg. Mar. 13th	$2,435	$1,702	$968	$4,500—Decorations	Regular priced Pre-Easter advertising

EVENT	PROMOTION DATE(S)	PRINT	RADIO	T.V.	EVENTS ON THE MALL	COMMENTS
After Easter Clearance	Beg. Apr. 7th	$1,489	$1,701	$ 720	_____	Start day after Easter
Mother's Day	Beg. May 1st	$1,263	$ 880	$ 720	$200—Gift Guide Booth	Regular priced Pre-Mother's Day advertising and Family Shopping Spree.
Father's Day	Beg. June 5th	$1,263	$ 880	$ 720		Regular priced Pre-Father's Day advertising and Family Shopping Spree
July Clearance	July 5th	$1,556	$1,293	$ 967	$667—Fire Works Display	Sale event starts July 5th
Sidewalk Sale	Aug. 1st	$ 513	$ 880	$ 720	$800—Booths	One-day event
Back-to-School	Aug. 7th	$1,556	$1,293	$967	$1,600—Safety Town	Regular priced Back-to-School advertising
Anniversary and Columbus Day Sale	Oct. 10th, 11th, 12th, 13th	$2,502	$1,622	$1,307	$1,753 —To be Scheduled	Four-day sale event
Sub Total **Production Cost** **TOTAL**		$23,646 3,160 $26,806	$19,644 2,809 $22,453	$13,827 1,783 $15,610	$21,842 ——— $21,842	$78,959 7,752 $86,711

APPENDIX D

Advertising Contract

Greater participation in every centerwide promotion by all Association members is fundamental, if they are to reach their volume potential. In many centers, a commitment to all special merchandise sections and/or cooperative pages is mandated by lease, although early leases do not have this clause. Therefore, to assure centerwide participation, the Board of Directors have devised a plan for prepaid advertising, which cost will be included in an increased dues structure.

Attached hereto, is a contract covering your commitment to this program, along with event-themes, dates, your space allocations in each publication, and the amount of your revised Merchants Association assessment.

To facilitate the planning and execution of your advertising and merchandise preparation, each event will be reconfirmed by fact sheet, at least four weeks prior to all ad deadlines. This will serve as a reminder, while allowing sufficient time for the preparation of your advertisements, merchandise, signs, etc.

This contract method, enthusiastically and unanimously approved by your Board of Directors, is being used successfully and profitably in many centers to assure merchant participation in center-sponsored promotions, where there is no covering lease provision. We ask your cooperation on this matter, which is important to the business health of every _____ merchant.

Please, therefore, sign and return the enclosed contract at your earliest convenience.

Cooperatively yours,

George Hixson

George Hixson
Promotion Director

*For use by centers without lease clauses for advertising

Merchants Association
Advertising and Promotion Contract

THIS AGREEMENT is made and entered into this _____ day of _____ , between _____ MERCHANTS ASSOCIATION hereinafter called "Association" and _____ hereinafter called "Member."
        (TENANT)

WITNESSETH:

That whereas, the parties hereto desire to conduct a general program of cooperative advertising and promotion at _____ for the period beginning _____
                        (MONTH AND YEAR)   (MONTH AND YEAR)

NOW THEREFORE, in consideration of the premises and other good and valuable considerations, the parties agree as follows:

1 Association agrees to spend a total of $ _____ for a program of cooperative advertising and promotion as shown on the accompanying schedule for said period.

2 Member agrees to pay to Association, as his proportionate share of the above total sum, $ total sum, $ _____ in four (4) equal installments of $ _____ all due and payable on or before the first day of each quarter. Upon receipt of the aforesaid payments thereof, Member shall be entitled to advertising space in the amount shown and in accordance with the attached "Schedule of Advertising Events," all without additional charge to Member; provided, however, that Member shall not be entitled to any further advertising in the event that Member is in default of his obligation hereunder or delinquent in making any of the aforementioned payments. Said advertising shall be placed in connection with Association's program of joint advertising and promotion for the year ending _____ 19xx

3 The deadline for receipt of all ads will be 14 days prior to insertion date, if preparation submitted requires proofs before publication, or 10 days prior to insertion date, if a complete mechanical requiring no proofs is submitted. A representative of Association's advertising agent will pick up all material at merchant's store on morning of deadline dates. In the event that said materials are not available at deadline date, Member shall not be entitled to place any advertising with Association for the subject insertion date unless Association's advertising agent permits a grace period in emergency cases. The aforementioned representative should be notified of tear sheet requirements for floor and window displays.

4 In the event that Member fails to pay any installments mentioned in Paragraph 2 hereof, or otherwise be in default of its obligations hereunder, in addition to its right to refuse Member the placement of additional advertising, the Association shall have the right to enforce collection of any delinquent payment by law. In the event that Member cures the default within 10 days from the date of the default, the member shall be entitled to reinstatement with full rights to place advertising with Association in connection with the execution of the balance of its program. Notice of default shall be deemed to have been properly given under this agreement when communicated orally to the company or its store manager at its place of business in Bel Air Shopping City.

In the event that Association, or its representative, negligently fail to place Member's advertising when timely delivered, Member may declare this contract null and void, in which event, Member shall be entitled to a refund of that portion of its quarterly payment that remains unexpended as determined by rated calendar days. If the failure to place said Advertising is not the fault of Association or its representatives, Member authorizes Association to hold that portion of Member's payment allocable to said unplaced advertising for use in connection with the further implementation of Association's program, as determined by the Board of Directors of the Association, it being understood that Association is a nonprofit organization of the Merchants and Owners of _____ and is pledged to use its best efforts toward the expenditure of Member's funds in the best interest of members and the Shopping City as a whole.

5 Association agrees to give to each member a full income and expense account of its operation for the fiscal year ending _____ , within 60 days after the close of the
 (DATE)
fiscal year. In the event that the total sum referred to in Paragraph 1 hereof is not collectible by or committed to Association by contracts with other members for the fiscal year ending _____ , Member agrees that Association's Advertising Committee shall be
 (DATE)
authorized to make such adjustments in the program as, in its sole discretion, it deems reasonable and just; provided, however, that in no event may advertising and promotion schedules, attached hereto, be changed without the consent of a majority of participating merchants.

6. Member warrants and represents that its execution hereof is fully authorized.

By _____
 Agent

By _____

_____
 Member

By _____

Schedule of Advertised Events

Event Theme	Promotion Date(s)	Proof Required	Deadline No Proof Required	*Your Prepaid Advertising Space
Election Day Specials	Nov. 6th	Oct. 22nd	Oct. 25th	_____
Pre-Christmas	Nov. 22nd	Nov. 8th	Nov. 13th	_____
Christmas	Dec. 18th	Dec. 4th	Dec. 8th	_____
After Christmas Clearance	Dec. 25th	Dec. 11th	Dec. 15th	_____
January Side Walk Sale	Jan. 24th Beg. 25th, 26th	Jan. 10th	Jan. 14th	_____
Washington's Birthday Sale	Feb. 16th, 17th, 18th	Feb. 2nd	Feb. 5th	_____
Spring Sale Days	Mar. 6th, 7th, 8th	Feb. 20th	Feb. 25th	_____
Easter	Beg. Mar. 13th	Feb. 27th	Feb. 25th	_____
After Easter Clearance	Beg. Apr. 7th	Mar. 24th	Mar. 27th	_____
Mother's Day	Beg. May 1st	Apr. 17th	Apr. 21st	_____
Father's Day	Beg. June 5th	May 22nd	June 26th	_____
July Clearance	Beg. July 5th	June 20th	June 24th	_____
Sidewalk Sale	Aug. 1st, 2nd	July 18th	July 22nd	_____
Back-to-School	Beg. Aug. 7th	July 24th	July 28th	_____
Anniversary Sale	Oct. 9th-13th	Sept. 25th	Sept. 29th	_____

*Event space dependent upon individual member's contribution to merchants association.

Assessment includes cost of advertising space (above).

Advertising Fact Sheet

Name of Event: _____

Date of Ad: _____

Event Days: _____

Name of Publication: _____

Mechanical Requirements: Column Width_____ Column Depth _____

Measurements (Above) _____ Before Processing _____ After Processing

Printing Process: _____ Offset _____ Letterpress

Deadline with Proof Required: _____

Deadline No Proof Required: _____

Cost: _____ Center Rate _____ Individual Merchant Contract Rate _____

Per Col.   Tabloid   ½ Tabloid   ¼ Tabloid

Inch _____   Page _____   Page _____   Page _____

Comments: _____

_____

_____

_____

Detach and mail to:

Please return on or before _____, _____

_____ Yes, we will advertise in the Bel Air Shopping City

_____on_____

   (NAME OF PUBLICATION)

Please reserve _____

_____ No, we will not advertise.

NAME _____

FIRM _____

DATE _____

INDEX